18 PAIR OF SHOES

18 PAIR
of
SH★ES

a memoir

Adventures of a Happiness Walker

PAULA FRANCIS

Haley's
Athol, Massachusetts

Haley's • 488 South Main Street • Athol, MA 01331
haley.antique@verizon.net • 978.249.9400

Photos from the collection of Paula Francis unless otherwise credited. Cover design by Paula Francis. Copy edited by Debra Ellis. Special thanks to Jessica Gale-Tanner.

Library of Congress Cataloging-in-Publication Data
Names: Francis, Paula, 1958- author.
Title: 18 pair of shoes / Paula Francis.
Other titles: 18 pairs of shoes
Description: Athol, Massachusetts : Haley's, [2022] | Summary: "Paula
    Francis reminisces about her ten-thousand-mile often solo
    circumambulation of the United States in seventeen legs between
2012 and
    2019 as the highlight of the project called Gross National Happiness
    USA. During the walk, Paula interviewed people all over the country
to
    find out their ideas of happiness. Although she sometimes received
    hospitality, she often camped out alone"-- Provided by publisher.
Identifiers: LCCN 2021055693 (print) | LCCN 2021055694 (ebook)
| ISBN
    9781948380522 (paperback) | ISBN 9781948380539 (hardcover) |
ISBN
    9781948380546 (kindle edition)
Subjects: LCSH: United States--Description and travel. | Francis, Paula,
    1958---Travel--United States. | Walking--United States. | Hiking--
United
    States. | Happiness--United States.
Classification: LCC E169.Z83 F684 2022 (print) | LCC E169.Z83
(ebook) |
    DDC 917.304--dc23/eng/20211116
LC record available at https://lccn.loc.gov/2021055693
LC ebook record available at https://lccn.loc.gov/2021055694

To all who have touched my life,
may you walk with beauty.

*When someone deeply listens to you, your bare feet are on the earth
and a beloved land that seemed distant is now home within you.*

—John Fox

When you know how to listen, everyone is a Guru.

—Baba Ram Dass

CONTENTS

ILLUSTRATIONS

A HAPPINESS ARCHITECT

a foreword by Christine A. Noyes

I slept through what could have been a defining moment in my life, and my sister Paula pens an account of it in *18 Pair of Shoes*. In my defense, I was two years old at the time. More than five decades dashed by before I completely understood the significance of my slumber. And it would be Paula who illuminated me.

Count me among many who did not understand why Paula felt compelled to walk around the country asking strangers, "What matters most in life?" My concerns were many. How would she stay safe? Where would she sleep? What would happen if she got hurt? And yes, where would she go to the bathroom?

But I can't say I felt surprised. Since childhood, Paula always searched for something. Her intense desire kept moving her forward to find new truths about the world and how we fit in it. I just didn't understand what she hoped to accomplish with her trek.

It wasn't until Paula reached Iowa, more than three-quarters of her journey complete, that our sister-in-law Mary and I joined her on the road . . . not to walk. No, no, no. That's not my thing. But to assist in getting her through the cornfields of middle America. Cerebrally, I knew the journey Paula had laid out for herself. I had a copy of the map and followed her progress. But in reality, seeing her day-to-day commitment firsthand blew my mind.

She woke early, donned her fanny pack, filled her water bottles, and, after breakfast in the Main Street diner, opened a dialogue with the owner and customers about what matters most in life. She then sat with a journalist from the local newspaper for an interview before walking twenty-eight miles, roughly ten hours—stopping along the way to interview strangers—to the next destination in the dry-dusty heat of the Heartland. That, Paula told us, constituted an easy day because she didn't need to haul her almost thirty-pound backpack or worry about where she would sleep that night. We transported her gear as we hopscotched along in our car and had planned overnight accommodations for the three of us. And that? Only one of her 896 days of The Happiness Walk.

Phew! I'm tired just thinking about it.

Paula opened up her vision of the world to me, and I found it fascinating. With confidence and fearlessness, she strides the streets at three miles an hour. Curious about the *serious about happiness* slogan on her blaze-orange safety vest, people seek her out. They expose their hearts and confess their most personal thoughts.

And Paula listens with empathy when needed, elation when called for, and thoughtfulness always. But never judgement.

I use the words confident and fearless to describe my sister, and she is certainly that. But that was not always the case. She had to work for it. It did not come naturally for her—or me—products of our tumultuous childhood. As evidenced by her walk, Paula's quest for truths is ongoing and has broadened in scope. She awakened a similar quest in me, just when I needed it most.

The United States Declaration of Independence guarantees all its citizens the unalienable right to the "pursuit of happiness." Unfortunately for many, it has become just that: the pursuit, the chase, the seeking of happiness. However, scholars tell us the original intent of the phrase does not mean the right to *pursue* happiness but to live *in* happiness, *practice* happiness, *catch* happiness. And it is up to each of us, individually, to choose to do so.

Paula has taught me to practice happiness. Now, imagine you can spread your happiness by simply speaking to your neighbor—a happiness pandemic so-to-speak. That, I understand now, is what my sister hoped and hopes to accomplish. Is there anything more important to humankind than that?

As you read the pages of Paula's book, you will be shocked, amused, saddened, and inspired. The stories she relays are our stories—our failures and our triumphs, our fears and our sureties, our pursuit of happiness.

I no longer dream through defining moments. I create them. I manifest my own happiness and try to infect others with it. I continue to move forward in learning truths about myself and my place in the universe. It has taken me almost sixty years to get here, and I can be a difficult student. But my sister never gave up on my education, my journey. She is tenacious that way. Who better to take on the herculean task of participating in changing the way we as a nation measure our health and well-being?

With her walk finished, Paula and I found ourselves binge-watching a cable network program called *The Good Place.* In Season Four, the character Eleanor finds herself in the unlikely position of assuming the role of architect of the afterlife neighborhood. Overwhelmed, she suggests she is not the right person for the job. "I can't do this. I am just a girl from Arizona," she states.

Michael, the real architect, responds, "Eleanor, the only one who *can* do this *is* a girl from Arizona."

Metaphorically speaking, Paula is a girl from Arizona who has happily worn out eighteen pair of shoes.

map created by Paula Francis

The Happiness Walk took place in increments through
Numbered circles on the route designated in green
A corresponding list of individual legs with named

seventeen legs from August 2012 to November 2019.
show a leg beginning and ending with a short black line.
starting and ending points appears on the following page.

Legs of the Happiness Walk
August 2012 to November 2019

Leg 1 • Stowe, Vermont to Washington DC
August 25 – October 10, 2012

Leg 2 • Stowe, Vermont to Montreal Canada
October 1 – October 8, 2013

Leg 3 • Washington, DC to Norfolk, Virginia
October 11 – 30, 2014

Leg 4 • Norfolk, Virginia to Raleigh, North Carolina
November 11 – 24, 2014

Leg 5 • Raleigh, North Carolina to Savannah, Georgia
January 15 – March 1, 2015

Leg 6 • Savannah, Georgia to Jacksonville, Florida
April 14 – May 6, 2015

Leg 7 • Jacksonville, Florida to Baton Rouge, Louisiana
September 9 – November 24, 2015

Leg 8 • Baton Rouge, Louisiana to Katy, Texas
January 26 – February 26, 2016

Leg 9 • Katy, Texas to Santa Fe, New Mexico
March 25 – June 2, 2016

Leg 10 • Santa Fe, New Mexico to Santa Monica, California
September 9 – November 19, 2016

Leg 11 • Santa Monica, California to San Francisco, California
October 2 – November 29, 2017

Leg 12 • Oahu, Hawaii
January 7 – 20, 2018

Leg 13 • San Francisco, California to Seattle, Washington
March 3 – May 13, 2018

Leg 14 • Seattle, Washington to Yakima, Washington
July 23 – August 7, 2018

Leg 15 • Yakima, Washington to Salt Lake City, Utah
September 19 – November 19, 2018

Leg 16 • Salt Lake City, Utah to Boston, Massachusetts
May 16 – November 2, 2019

Leg 17 • Silent Walk from Deerfield, Massachusetts to
Montpelier, Vermont
November 12 – 19, 2019

JUMPING TIMELINES

a preface by Paula Francis

My walkabout took place over the course of seven years—sometimes on the road, sometimes off. In total, adding together walking days, I actively engaged in the Happiness Walk for roughly two and one-half years or 896 days to be exact from 2012 to 2019.

The story of the journey jumps timelines over long distances like a kangaroo on hot desert sand. To help orient you to my travels, the map on the page before the list of legs of the walk indicates my entire walking route. With few exceptions, after I completed a leg, I took a break and then returned to where I left off to continue my journey forward.

I methodically connected each step to the next as I circumambulated the country in route segments or legs. It can be difficult to live up to one's self-imposed standards. Sometimes, especially when another person walked with me, I formulated creative solutions to walking long days without a support vehicle. Perhaps we or I walked in reverse from the day's destination to the desired starting point for reasons typically related to lodging availability. I rarely had support vehicles during my time on the road. When one did appear, added help and welcomed shedding of my backpack not only lightened my load but my attitude.

In all, during my calculated 21,504 hours on the road and estimated 23,569,000 steps I took, people routinely treated me with kindness and generosity. Countless strangers offered meals, housing, rides, and emotional support. I mention some two hundred representative people in the following pages.

Even as I experienced its wonderment and even as each rising sun brought a new sense of aliveness, I would never suggest any part of the walk was easy. Each leg took long and careful planning, each day required pluck and grit, and each hour stretched my body, mind, and spirit to their limits. My feet calloused, my shoulders and back ached, my skin burned, and my insides thirsted much of the time.

It was not easy.

But it was phenomenal.

The hardships are not what linger. In actuality and in an odd and somewhat cleansing way, I welcomed them. They chipped away false reflections of myself to lay bare what I needed to discover in order to live life more honestly and fully. And the chiseling is not complete. Each cut seems to reveal a deeper lesson. I remain a work in progress that shifts with each fresh understanding and every new insight.

To paraphrase Yogi Berra, "I'm taking it all with a grin of salt because the future ain't what it used to be."

THE HAPPINESS WALKER

an introduction by Paula Francis

People like the thought of me, the Happiness Walker traveling around the country on foot. With a glimpse at my costume, they see what they want to see. And since this undertaking is less about me and much more about them, I reveal little. They paint in details to their liking, and the Technicolor character they fashion projects much larger than the one inside me. My anonymity somehow invites their favor. Hearts are bared and secrets made visible. I, however, remain unexposed in their spotlight: a comfortable way of being. But the curtain is closing, and there's only one curtain call.

November 2, 2019

I stroll past Fenway Park, down Commonwealth Avenue Mall, and onto Boston Common, America's oldest public park, clocking in at 9,861 miles, the completion of my listening project. As with many milestones around the country, this one, too, is anticlimactic. Though I have a small parade of friends and family who travel far and wide to celebrate the long-awaited

1

moment with me, the day is awash in gray. I'm not exactly sure what I am feeling, but I brace against it and posture, smiling and toasting and cajoling in camaraderie, never revealing my tears are not of joy.

I've worn this costume so long—walking shoes, safety vest, recorder in my pocket—I'm not sure what I'll find when I peel it off. I will no longer be The Walker. I'll simply be Paula, indistinguishable from every other person navigating the planet: a mother of grown daughters, a divorcee without a home or job or car, a woman without her next plan. For someone who's comfortable with the unknown, these details now weigh on me. After all, it's time to digest the enormity of what I've just done, and on this afternoon in November—I've just outgrown my tent.

November 19, 2019

The ten-day-long celebration and much needed rest nearly dissipates the gloom. It is cold but sunny as I retrace my steps from the inaugural walk of seven years ago back up to Vermont where my adventure began and where Gross National Happiness USA was birthed.

Though conscientious to assure that my interviews reflect the great diversity within the country, there remain—even with laborious effort—people whose voices are underrepresented in my happiness research. Unsurprisingly, they include those who are systemically unheard, disenfranchised, disregarded, hidden, and silenced: in other words, those unlikely to be happy. And while I make earnest attempts to speak with people in a variety of settings, interviews do not adequately represent people who are institutionalized nor those for whom either my communication skills or my route posed barriers. In recognition of that paucity, I walk the remaining 139 miles of the 10,000-mile trek in silence. My last leg of the Happiness Walk is strictly a personal one.

My sister Chris Noyes acts as my support vehicle and while together, I often falter in my silence with habitual thank yous, where's the bathroom, and what's the forecast. But it's easy not to engage in random conversation as I tread the snowy Vermont roads in seven-degree weather with every bit of me under winter cover. I keep a notepad for important written communications, which are few, but it comes in handy for orders of hot, dark roast coffee at layovers calculated to defrost my fingers and toes.

I'm comfortable in the silence. I prefer it. My feelings, though, remain elusive. This is new territory, and my incoherent emotions and I need to get better acquainted before they share their names. Eventually, without a true sense of where it is, I make my way closer to center.

I've read that while on Earth we carry the wounds of our ancestors. I like to think that, along my travels, I've unloaded many parcels of my ancestors' pain from my backpack. Perhaps that accounts for the emptiness I feel. Or maybe it's the nakedness underneath my garb, or even yet, the prospect of a new wound, one where the project is an empty promise. While I'm satisfied knowing I've given all I could to the Happiness Walk, apparently my ego continues to require a roadmap towards an opportune exit.

December 3, 2008

Let me back up a bit. Allow me to travel in reverse to the year I happened upon a different type of map, one that put me on this anomalous course in the first place.

Linda Wheatley and I ran into one another as we were picking our kids up from school. She was just back from the Fourth International Gross National Happiness Conference in Thimphu, Bhutan, a place I would visit years later. She didn't have to say much, but I was bowled over by the idea of using happiness as a yardstick for measuring national progress. Within a week, we were planning an international conference of our own in our home state of Vermont, and shortly thereafter, she and I jumped right into co-founding GNHUSA with a small group of old and new friends.

We began the endeavor at a time when George W. Bush announced a seven-hundred-billion-dollar bailout package for big banks—a full year into a deepening economic recession. It was also the year that Bhutan, the architect of Gross National Happiness, officially became the world's newest democracy. Several years later, GNH is a paradigm taking hold across the globe with excellent examples of happiness policies evident within Scandinavian countries. Along with its widespread adoption emerges a sweeping and positive movement towards greater justice, equity, harmonic living, and naturally, happiness: where people matter over profit.

Gross National Happiness USA. First of all . . . Gross? Okay, I understand that's not sexy. Believe me, there have been many discussions about changing that language, but you have to take it into context with the countering view of Gross National Product. That term, undoubtedly, came from a left-brain-person, not a dreamer like me. I'm simply pointing out, we didn't make up the name. Furthermore, others around the world have adopted the lingo so we, too, at GNHUSA fell in line.

Happiness. Now that's a notion we can all get our heads around—sort of. We each may have a slightly different idea of what happiness is, but in general, we know it is something good, and we tend to all want it. The real question is what is *gross happiness*? Can we really apply it as a measure similar to how we use a gross product? Can policies and practices be built around an inexorably vague concept? Finally, can happiness possibly be legislated? Better yet, do we want it to be?

Well, yes and yes and sort of!

Whether we like it or not, whether we know it or not, we bring into our consciousness the things we measure—it's quantum mechanics. I'd love to get into that (because I love the science of it all), but it wouldn't suit my purpose here very well. Practically speaking, if I valued the quality of my interactions with people along my Happiness Walk, my pace suffered due to time spent in conversation. If instead I measured success as the number of miles I walked, speed became my focus, and the quality and quantity of my interactions diminished.

We get what we put our minds to so what we pay attention to matters!

As far back as 1968 in a speech at the University of Kansas, Senator Robert Kennedy discussed the colossal pitfalls of a myopic focus on our Gross National Product, GNP, saying we

> have surrendered personal excellence and commu-
> nity values [to] the mere accumulation of material
> things. . . [GNP] measures neither our wit nor our
> courage, neither our wisdom nor our learning, neither
> our compassion nor our devotion to our country, it
> measures everything in short, except that which makes
> life worthwhile.

He further elucidated, it can tell us everything about America except why we are proud that we are Americans. And that's where the USA in Gross National Happiness USA comes in.

So, what are our values? What truly makes life worthwhile? How do we measure answers to these questions? These are inquiries a GNHUSA paradigm considers. And here, then, is the genesis of the Happiness Walk. Rather than traveling down the timeworn road of more growth and stuff as measured within a GNP-based blueprint, GNHUSA urges an alternative byway that cultivates fertile conditions for our collective happiness. At the very core of the concept is the importance of raising up the voices of *We the People*, and the walk—with its thousands of interviews—is a means to tap into that voice.

Of course, it is much more nuanced than the ideas raised here, but in my view—and in the view of many others much more learned than I—the choice is clear. Given the current conditions of our economic, health, ecological, social, governmental, judicial, and educational systems, we need a new North Star. I believe a GNH compass can guide us in a more prosperous and principled direction leading to drawing of new maps.

To cite Bruce Nichols, a host and new friend in Shelton, Connecticut: "I think richness is not measured by the size of your bank account but measured more by the size of your heart and your capacity to love and care for others."

Bruce verbalizes what I hear so frequently from people across this land: money isn't everything. According to my research, it isn't even close. And while people may define happiness in varying degrees, it is extraordinary how similar our basic values are. I know a little something about it not because I'm scholarly, but because I walked around this beautiful, complex, diverse, and promising country listening for the answer to the question "What matters most in life?"

When I have a moment to re-listen to recordings of interviews I conducted, the conversations conjure up a range of emotions: some happy, some sad, all of them raw and real. There are more than three thousand such recordings, all of them eventually analyzed by some of the best data-driven minds in applied research at the University of Vermont Center for Rural Studies in Burlington.

Bottom-line: Bruce gets it right. Relationships are what we value most. We care greatly about our connections to people as well as to animals, and we also care deeply about the planet. Incongruously and tragically, it is easy to witness the shameless dismissals of individual and wholesale suffering of people, the extinction of animals, and the degradation of our planet, a colossal failure in morality played out before our eyes. It will not do. It is time to act as the powerful, creative, and enterprising people we are.

We have a choice. As my good friend and fellow GNHUSA colleague Ginny Sassaman likes to ask, "Are you willing to feed your happiness dog?" That is a loose reference to a famous indigenous American story about two wolves. One wolf holds the attributes of anger, contempt, fear, shame, and hate. The other wolf embraces the qualities of gratitude, inspiration, awe, serenity, and love. A child asks his Cherokee grandfather, "Which wolf wins?"

Grandfather's answer, "The one you feed."

"Happiness is not something you have to earn. It's not something some people can have and some people can't. I think it's a choice," says Emily Galligan of West Tisbury, Massachusetts. "I think too many people see it as, well, 'It is what it is, and I just have to suck it up and deal with it.' That's not so. If people could realize they have a choice, it really is that simple. And once you have a little taste for it, you realize you can keep making that choice, and it makes a huge difference in your life."

It surely makes a difference in my life. People ask me, "Why did you walk?" and my simple answer is, "I walked because I desire for all people to be happy." My greatest fear in life is to not contribute, to live without striving to make a positive difference in some way. I feel the walk was my calling, my undeniable purpose for the moment.

Saskia walked a few miles with me into Washington, DC, "If you are blessed to some extent with a very comfortable life, you should constantly challenge yourself to see that if there's injustice somewhere," she says, "it will affect you, too." Saskia sees the interconnectedness of us all. She understands that service to others is a high order. Like Saskia, I prefer that uplifting way over service to self.

So, can happiness be legislated? It's unlikely. But, with constitutions of loving hearts, we can create policies and manage expectations that clear the debris from our way so our lives can flourish and allow happiness to prevail. "It is not easy to practice love, friendship, generosity, understanding, or solidarity within a system whose rules, goals, and information streams are geared for lesser human qualities," writes Donella Meadows in *Limits to Growth*. "But we try." We can steer towards our own individual pleasures or choose to harmonize in a flotilla of happiness. The choice is ours. The dog we feed matters.

Challenged by the physical rigor of the walk, the emotional brawn required, the unrelenting spiritual fortitude entailed, I am glad to report that I have more faith in humanity today than when I first became a wayfarer. In a purely personal context, the journey was so very worthwhile. I cannot think of much I could have—should have—done up to this point in my life to bring me as much meaning and contentment. In spite of the fleeting feeling of emptiness—or because of it—I am satiated.

An anthropologist proposed a game to some children in an African community. He put a basket full of fruit near a tree and said whoever got to the tree first would win the sweet fruits. When he told the children to run, they took one another's hands, ran together, and then sat down to enjoy their treats. When asked why they ran as one when each could have captured all the fruits, the children replied, "Ubuntu, how can one of us be happy if all the other ones are not?"

Dear reader, my happiness is inextricably linked to yours. Since the final steps of the Happiness Walk, I have learned to walk happily through life without sneakers, and I pledge to continue to do my unselfish part to create my own happiness—for your sake. Conversely, your happiness is inevitably linked to mine. I hope you, too, take steps towards creating a full and happy life for the sake of all others, that we may enjoy the bountiful fruits of this Earthly basket we weave together.

Ubuntu—I am because we are.

Now, a little about this book.

This book is not a project of GNHUSA. What I write here does not necessarily reflect the views of the organization nor the people involved. It is my reflection on lessons both personal and professional I learned along my walk. I have tried to stay true to GNHUSA's core values, but I am quite aware—and the reader should be, too—that my own biases are on full display.

While I began writing about the results of the Happiness Walk, with my experiences in life as the backdrop, somewhat surprisingly this book became more about my life's journey with the Happiness Walk as my backdrop. If it is data and research you seek, this is not the book for you. I'll spare you the effort of reading and point you to the chapter entitled "Lean Into the Wind" where I touch upon the results of my research.

While I asked those I interviewed for their consent to share their stories, I'm guessing no one anticipated—not even me—being the focus of a book. For that reason, I changed the names of a few people so as to give as much anonymity as possible unless I have been given specific permissions. I may have made minor changes to quotes for grammatical or clarifying purposes to assist the reader but never to alter the intent of unamended transcriptions.

And then there's me.

I tend to be a rather private person. I rarely share details of my life, and the tendency proved more true while on my seven-year walkabout. Even my good friends gently chide me for keeping my thoughts and feelings so close to my chest. But here, on these pages, I expose myself in a vulnerable and, yes, uncomfortable way. If we've met, some of you may be surprised by what you read while others may have seen right through me. Either way, I feel I must explain three things.

First, I am neither Catholic, Buddhist, nor affiliated with any formal religious institution. I subscribe to many spiritual teachings, some that may seem too restrictive and others too metaphysical. The upshot is that I honor everyone's purely held beliefs. In the pages that follow, I have capitalized an array of names used to denote an Infinite Creator of any sort. Please do not read into the limited mentions of divine beings or spiritual leanings. My pages are finite though Divinity is not.

My second reveal is related to my first. You will notice I capitalize Earth because I also hold our planet sacred. I view our Earth as a living entity—Gaia, a deity in her own right.

Last and most important, if you tend to process events chronologically as do most people, be forewarned you may become dizzy from the sequencing of my memoir. It will take you from one year to the next and back to the past before it catapults you into the future once more. Much as a seeker in a labyrinth explores a western orientation even while winding towards the center to the east, I explore stories from the ebb and flow of time while moving closer to my truth as I understand it today. I pay little attention to the construct of time. I am more interested in the evolution of life than the progression of the sundial.

Take your Dramamine pill now!

Locales along the Happiness Walk include,
from left to right, top to bottom,
Quebec, Canada • Frelighsburg, Quebec • Phoenix, Arizona
Oxnard, California • Los Olivos, California • Cleveland, Ohio
Jackson, Michigan • Jacksonville, Florida • Winthrop Harbor, Illinois,
Day, Florida • Sante Fe, New Mexico • Santa Monica, California
San Louis Obispo, California • Craig, Colorado • Kearney, Nebraska
Aurelian Springs, North Carolina • Wellsville, New York • Honolulu, Hawaii

PARALLEL JOURNEYS

Don't stumble over something behind you.

—Seneca the Younger
Roman philosopher

He pulls his truck over and keeps it running while offering good wishes for my journey. I tug at the backpack that rode my lap and jump the several feet from the tractor trailer to the waiting shoulder of the road. I don't know him, but as he drives away, an unfamiliar heaviness overcomes me.

What the hell am I doing?

February 8, 2016
30.2360°N 92.8226°W
Welsh, Louisiana

Unlikely tears begin to form, and I force them into retreat. I am left alone on the side of the road in the small town of Welsh, Louisiana, hometown of the Swamp Pop legend Charles Mann who mocks me with his rendition of "Walk of Life." It's 2016, and I have incrementally traveled twenty-five hundred miles on foot on similar roads the past few years, but there are times when loneliness grabs me.

Why the hell am I here?

No one knows where I am. If I went missing, days could go by and no one would be the wiser. Typically, rural roads are welcome by me—and I know they will be again in another mile. I just need to push through intruding doubts, pull in the fresh air, and put one foot in front of the other. That's how I got from my home in Vermont to here, and that's how I'll get back.

What the hell was I thinking?

I left what most people would consider a very comfortable life for one entirely uncertain and, likely for most people, scary. And that would be correct for me as well if I didn't have higher expectations for growing into my true self. I left my work, my home, and eventually my marriage. My girls also left—as they should have. They are grown and rooted in their own lives. The only person I feel truly remiss in leaving behind is my aging father, though I return frequently to spend precious weeks with him.

I am away for several months at a time on the Happiness Walk, following in the footsteps of indigenous desert Indians, Peace Pilgrim, and Forrest Gump. I am on a quest not only to live out my calling but also to save ourselves from ourselves as a nation by shifting our way of thinking about success and progress from a narrow measure of economics towards a barometer of life-enriching conditions. My mission is bold because my vision is bold. And it all plays out one small step at a time.

Who do I think I am?

My life's pattern has been to give myself over to the charge of others. I believed that putting my own needs and desires aside was an act of generosity and righteousness. I was misguided. I suffered, but I accepted that as my life's story. Until I imploded. I felt caged, invisible, and spiritually stunted. I was not being me. As Brent of Portland, Oregon said, "You can wear happiness pajamas to bed, but it doesn't mean you're going to become happy. It has got to be inside you."

It's no wonder people didn't see the struggle within me. All they saw were my pajamas.

Most of my family was understandably surprised by the news of the end of my twenty-seven-year marriage, though my daughters were not. Other family members were truly perplexed by my unorthodox need to literally walk into a new life, though my daughters were not—they share a lot of my genes.

I began walking a year after my mother's death on my fifty-fourth birthday in August of 2012. The inaugural walk of 600-miles from Stowe, Vermont, to Washington DC turned into a ten-thousand-mile odyssey. Seven weeks turned into seven years. A relatively short trek became an expedition of my soul.

I have circumambulated the country through thirty-two states and over the border into Canada. Beginning in 2012, I walked from Montpelier, Vermont, to Jacksonville, Florida (avec un rapide voyage de 180 kilometers à travers la frontière Canadienne à Montréal), west to Santa Monica, where I dipped my calloused toes into the Pacific Ocean before heading north to Seattle and finally back east to Boston, by way of the Corn Belt. A crowning trip in silence to Vermont culminated my walk on November 19, 2019.

More than that, the walk has taken me places I never could have planned emotionally, physically, and spiritually. Though the Happiness Walk was fundamentally a project of Gross National Happiness USA, or GNHUSA, it was also a personal pilgrimage. I am humbled to have been on the listening end of people's stories. At the same time, it was exciting to be creating my own.

As these thoughts swirl through the first mile of my day in Welsh, I notice Southwestern Louisiana is missing correctional facilities and military bases I've become used to along my coastal route since Virginia, though it is still dotted with casinos and oil fields. I am adept at recognizing the sounds of large Confederate flags fluttering from the back of Dodge pickup trucks behind me alerting me to their approach and affording me safe navigation along shoulderless streets.

People honk and wave as they pass me in my construction-orange walking vest with the slogan of the Happiness Walk reading *serious about happiness*. As usual, the interviews with locals are touching at Rabideaux's Sausage Kitchen twelve miles into my day in Iowa, Louisiana—I won't reach the state of Iowa for three more years. The town is home to the annual Iowa Rabbit Festival capped off with a Petite Lapin Pageant. Contrary to my initial belief and wish that it honors the life of the adorable, long-eared, fluffy creatures, it gives me pause to learn it celebrates the town's rabbit processing plant.

Approaching Lake Charles, I stop at *America Press* for an impromptu interview that gets me on the top fold of the back of the front section of the paper, a real coup in a small city for my mission. It is one of my longer days at twenty-nine miles—sunny with strong headwinds. And while I've told myself I would never walk in the dark again after my as-yet-to-be-told experience in Florida, I do. And I do again two and three days later. Winter daylight is not my friend: it arrives late and rudely excuses itself before dinner.

Though the end of a lengthy day's walk is rewarding, it is not the end of my day. I make a call to check on Marilyn Bush who broke her arm just days before in Lafayette on her final day of walking with me. Into my running tally of expenses and donations, I log my non-rabbit lunch at Rabideaux's and the twenty dollars given me by Linda Lu—in all her colorful Fat Tuesday garb.

I was gifted a night's lodging at the L'Auberge Casino and Resort—a complete luxury! After a large salad (get the greens when you can) at Jack Daniel's Bar and Grill and a failed attempt to participate in a GNHUSA board conference call, I make plans for crossing the I-10 bridge, which a sheriff tells me is the only route possible though illegal to pedestrians. I research possibilities for home stays or other overnights for the following couple of days and finally, settle into the comfy hotel bed at 11:30 where I write in my journal and watch the New Hampshire pre-game: the 2016 presidential primaries. I am exhausted yet anticipating tomorrow's rare day off from walking to attend local Mardi Gras celebrations.

Several months later, there I am watching the presidential debates back home in Vermont. I soon won't own a house once the divorce papers get processed. I have no use for the car or the many items I own jointly with my husband. I'm not yet clear what I will do after the walk is over or where I will be, though I am curious to see what will unfold. My present needs are nominal. I desire only the essential things I can carry, the generosity and care of strangers, and the magic the universe provides.

I've come home in a brand-new way. And while not there yet, through the Happiness Walk I am coming home to myself. And so commences another voyage of discovery, one that's exclusively by me for me. Though one did not cause the other, the two are intertwined. This is the story of those parallel journeys . . . both for the sake of happiness.

Paula interviews a vendor at the Santa Fe Indian Market on September 26, 2016 at 3,591 miles during Leg 10 of the Happiness Walk.

LEAN INTO THE WIND

In a culture of distraction, be a revolutionary.

—Mat Wyble
Panama City, Florida

Mudslides, missiles, and mountain lions will be a few of my teachers on this excursion. But today, on a national day of observance in Macclenny, Florida, I am a student of Danny.

September 11, 2015
30.28822°N 82.1221°W
Macclenny, Florida

Danny Thicke's daughter overslept and missed her flight on September 11, 2001. Fourteen years later, he recounts that moment to Ginny Sassaman and me as we eat our thickly syruped pancakes at yet another Waffle House along the Happiness Walk. He has a heap of stories, and we hear a good many of them as he kindly delivers us 3.5 miles down the road to Glen St. Mary while holding his tiny Chihuahua in his lap.

He points to the surrounding prisons—of which there are many—and we learn about the time he was fired from his position as a correctional officer for knifing a detainee after following the inmate into an enclosed yard. "Mostly, I had very respectful relationships with the prisoners," he proudly boasts, "but he deserved it. The Blacks are like apes. They are violent except if you're with them one on one. They play on one another's aggression." The Reverend William Barber II, whom I met while walking through Virginia, sees it differently. He refers to prisons as the new lynching trees.

It is difficult to listen to Danny's prejudices, but as I'm forming my reply, he makes an abrupt U-turn in the middle of the two-lane road, drives over the sidewalk, and comes to a full stop on the grassy yard of the *Lake City Reporter.*

Danny was orphaned for the first five years of his life, and he still harbors regret for not reaching out to a lost boy he once saw. "I should have brought him home with me, took care of him," he says with distant eyes as he slowly shakes his head, perhaps recalling his own neglected childhood. He talks tenderly of his puppies, Man and Doodlebug. We hear about his many acts of goodwill. Heck, we are the recipients of one.

That is a typical start to a day on the road, ripe with contradictions and challenges but always, always an opportunity to learn. I am here to listen—not to judge but to understand. So I listen intently and ask good questions. I stay curious. It is all fodder for reflection during the many long and silent stretches of road yet to come.

Not for nothing, Ginny and I remain immensely grateful to Danny. Retracing steps to our starting point in the morning would have added another hour to our day, and we couldn't afford it—in time or energy. We thank him for the ride and crawl out from under the piles of junk mail and tools stored permanently in his truck onto the lawn of a local newspaper, where we will tell our story. As we wave goodbye, we say we hope to see him for breakfast the next morning, which we do.

Ginny, another co-founder of GNHUSA, has joined the research project for a few days. When we meet people, we expect to interview them about happiness. That typically leads to a broad array of topics preoccupying people's minds, thus offering our organization a rich reserve of information we draw on for our policy work. Interviews take place in almost every kind of place you can imagine, including fishing holes, nursing homes, alligator farms, barbershops, tribal offices, cornfields, houseboats, homeless communities, toll booths, doughnut shops, public bathrooms, police cars, and, routinely, on the sides of the street. Today they take place on Route 90.

Ginny and I get on the road a little later than hoped, which becomes a common theme. We leave our backpacks in the musty Motel 6 room where we will return after we make our miles. It's a comfort to know we have a place to rest our heads tonight even though it's money out of our pockets and a relief to walk twenty-eight pounds lighter than usual. I wear the neon t-shirt that reads FREEDOM my sister Chris made for me and carry only what I need for the day: my phone, phone battery, hand wipes, hand lotion, lip balm, handkerchief, voice recorder, and wallet with ID, credit cards, and minimal cash— no coins: they are too weighty.

Down the road a short way, a single man in a parked car fervently waves us over. I'm reluctant to approach. However, my reluctance is not because of the man but due to the large pit bull poking his head out the driver's side window. I've had run-ins with pit bulls, and the trauma has not yet subsided. Phil recognizes us from last night's local broadcast news. He wants to chat about his recent stroke and how his newly acquired talent as an oil painter helps in his recovery. Knowing that we are interested in his happiness, he is sincere and eager to share. We listen as earnestly as we can while swatting mosquitoes buzzing around our heads. Several miles later, he catches up with us after he's traveled nine miles out to a local pharmacy and back so as to gift us with two enormous bottles of much-needed bug repellent. They double the weight we carry, but the burden of mosquitoes is lessened.

Midday, relieved to find anything there at all, we stop for lunch in a one-store, one-bar town. Stripes convenience stores have sufficed for restaurant and bathroom stops in this remote area, so finding a small market is a score. We grab some bruised fruits and processed cheese and, with upturned plastic crates as chairs and another for a table, we take the liberty of dining contentedly on the back loading dock, resting our tired feet, unmoved by the odors emanating from adjacent dumpsters.

All throughout the day, cars beep as we wave. It's fun to be recognized. The wave factor increases a day or two following a television broadcast or news article, and we bask in the wake. We aren't prepared, though, for the car that races directly at us, horn blasting, with a couple hanging out their respective windows pointing and screaming "It's them. I think it's them!" They jerk the car off the road, park in our tracks, jump out, and ask excitedly, "Are you the happiness ladies?" while seamlessly extending a selfie stick for a photo op.

"You will be the talk of the barbershop for days," says the female stylist who had her husband make an illegal U-turn after she spied us.

I sure hope so, I say to myself. We will soon be in need of a host in that particular town. I'll hedge my bets and keep my eyes out for someone with a recent buzz cut.

A few towns and a day later, notice of our arrival bumps news of Pope Francis's upcoming visit off the front page, above the fold of the *Lake City Reporter*. My apologies to the Pope, though in a 2014 interview, he imparted his top ten happiness secrets to the masses, so I think he would approve.

Television and radio spots are great ways to reach a broader audience about the mission of the Happiness Walk. While my experience reinforces people's disillusionment regarding the editorial, repetitive, and sensational nature of news cycles, we're having good traction on the seventh leg of the walk. Over the course of the project, I will find small-to-medium sized towns far more receptive to coverage than cities, and it's a bonus when stories are mostly correct or print anything other than the number of miles I've walked or how many pair of shoes I've worn.

The *Lake City Reporter* is one of the welcomed exceptions in that the reporters are informed, intrigued, ask relevant questions, and report accurately. It's regretful that Danny chewed up their grassy lawn as he dropped us at their doorstep, though I don't say that to his face when we meet over breakfast the following morning in need of yet another ride to our starting point.

Walking with me for the first eleven days of seven-hundred-seventy-five steamy miles from Jacksonville to Baton Rouge, Ginny and another Vermonter will join me there for a few more. In her sixties, Marilyn arrives with two intact arms and leaves with her left arm in a sling in her seventies. Her seventieth birthday turns out to be one of the unfortunate mishaps on the walkabout.

I travel alone for the vast majority of my cumulative miles. However, over the course of the journey, I am joined by ninety-seven walkers who accompany me for as little as fifty feet, as my Uncle George proudly did with the aid of his walker less than a year before his passing, and up to several hundred miles with people you will meet as I tell my tale about the walk. For more than eight thousand miles, waves of passersby, the honks of the eight-wheelers, and the whistles of the trains meet my needs for companionship.

Alone or not, people around the country greet me with great enthusiasm. Their answers are recorded, and within a year, I and others have transcribed, coded, and analyzed all three-thousand-plus. Responses vary, of course, but not as much as you might think. Ultimately, GNHUSA will use the information to determine societal conditions that support our happiness and well-being and work to shift US public policy accordingly.

You see, happiness arises from attending to what matters, to what gives life meaning. What people report matters most in life is worthy of our collective conversation. Those are the things we ought to preserve diligently—or, better yet—enhance.

So in the span of a couple of days in Florida, I am affirmed in my purpose for walking. I witness the juxtaposition between declarations of what matters most—relationships, love, meaning, spirituality, lifelong learning, caring for one another, health, peace, the natural world, and time to pay attention to what we value and their incompatible societal manifestations—loneliness, poverty, violence, food deserts, pollution, and xenophobia. There's a great divide between what we say matters and how we live our lives. It appears we've become complacent, forgoing our personal potential for the promise of mediocrity and settling on "comfortable enough" and "safe enough" rather than on "thriving"—or worse, unconsciously outsourcing our power for others to usurp for their own purposes.

My curiosity regarding the phenomenon of abdicating our will for indifference is best captured by Marta Ceroni of Norwich, Vermont who asks, "How is it and why is it that we individually desire and strive for certain very important goals for ourselves, but at the same time, we design systems far from what we really want?" The consequences can be dire, I might add.

I, too, question how is it, why is it that we share some very common values across age, gender, race, ethnicity, socioeconomics, geography, religions, and politics, yet we hear over and over again how very different we are? As evidenced in my findings, we consistently portray ourselves as a fractured society whose very humanity is often called into question. From where does all that vitriol stem—and who benefits? Where are unifying messages? Where is public discourse where we talk out our differences without fear of contempt or condemnation?

"I know of no safe repository of the ultimate power of society but the people," Thomas Jefferson said. It is clear within the first hundred miles of my multi-year campaign that, broadly speaking, people don't feel powerful—nor, for that matter, heard. That view magnifies as the years pass, thus amplifying a blanket of apathy in 2012, frustration in the twenty-teens, and outright anger in 2019. I submit that the culminating social and political discord springs from impotence seeded so many years ago within our systems. Without proper attitudes of intellectual inquiry, dialog, engagement, and discernment, that blight spirals downward and entangles its roots into people's conceptualization of what they see as reality when, in actuality, our complicity is our undoing.

I walked through three presidential election cycles over seven years. President Barack Obama sat in the White House as I took my first steps in August of 2012. A contentious campaign reigned as I walked through the South in 2016 as another did in 2019 while I transited the North on my return trip to New England. I've walked through every kind of political storm as inflaming rhetoric flooded the airways with minute-by-minute news of their destructive paths. Hardly ever, in all those years, have I beheld the political promise of a rainbow.

November 9, 2016
34.1347°N, 116.3131°W
Joshua Tree, California

I am shielded from much of the controversy and gaming of the 2016 presidential campaign both by choice and by virtue of walking the widths of Texas, New Mexico, and Arizona that limit my access to 24/7 news. I step out of my tent on a cold November morning after crossing the Mojave Desert. I am still exhausted yet eager to learn results of the election, but I need caffeine even more.

As I take a seat in the crowded Starbucks, I can't help but notice the woman sitting two tables away. She sobs uncontrollably as people rotate in and out of an adjacent chair in an attempt to console her. She is obviously devastated by the results of the election, and I'm rather surprised at her shock. I've trekked every mile of the country from Vermont to Joshua Tree, California, and it feels plausible that President Donald Trump would be chosen as our next leader for the very reasons I have enumerated: people do not feel heard, and their needs are not being met through the very systems put in place to uplift them. Plus, they are embittered by disingenuous career politicians. It looks obvious to me the electorate would choose a political outsider. If only people could hear what I hear.

Now what I'm engaged in is not a political walk. I am simply observing and reflecting on what I'm told. I seek to support a better, happier life for everyone and do not promote one candidate over another, one group of people over another, nor one issue over others. But it is clear to me that we've cultivated a dependency on undependable systems, and unless we have leaders who are honest, fair, transparent, bold, and willing to create systems that invest in life rather than money, there will exist a lack of trust in whomever sits in high office.

Personally, I am politically homeless. I do not label my political beliefs, nor do I sit comfortably on either side of the aisle. I am put off by any urging to define ourselves as either round or square pegs when we actually express ourselves in so many other shapes. I consider it a triumph when people I interview bring up politics, which they unfailingly do, and assume their political leanings are mine. Truth is, I lean into a point of view like I lean into the desert wind—it's the only way I can master the release of judgment. It's the only way for me to ground in compassion. It's the only way I want to be. I might get scorched by the pavement, I may lose footing on a rocky shoulder, but the road leads us all to the same place once we see beyond the division and distractions seemingly placed in our path.

So, as I join thousands of people in the process of refocusing our attention onto conditions of happiness and well-being, it makes sense to have a clear understanding of what that means in practice. What is true for us in the United States may be somewhat different from what is true for people who reside in other countries around the globe, I therefore thought it important to ask for the views of *We the People of the United States,* an endeavor that defines my route cause for walking and the purpose for recording and separately publishing what I have found.

And while my literal destination remains constant from day to day, mile to mile, and state to state, I have no idea where my epiphanies will guide me. It's a map I'm creating as I go.

Paula's late mother, Joyce Johnson in 2001, was "beautiful, eccentric, playful, compassionate, and loving," says Paula.

WARRIOR

I choose to have my personality serve my soul.
—Cynthia Stibolt
Santa Fe, New Mexico

I prepare like a decorated soldier for the logistics, the elements, and uncertainties of my multi-year undertaking, yet I am unprepared for the battle waged by constant chatter in my head. Ruthless minefields sure to subvert any semblance of serenity seed my mind. Ultimately, those chattering voices constitute my greatest challenge—not the blisters on my feet that first week in Woodstock, Vermont, that had me crawling on the floor of F. H. Gillingham and Sons General Store in search of a remedy for throbbing pain. It is not the 108-degree heat blow-torching my lungs in Big Springs, Nebraska. It isn't even drunk Bernie who reaches over to rub my leg as he gives me a ride and brags about his daily trips to Panama City's strip clubs.

No, it is my monkey mind that proves the most cunning and capable saboteur of peace, an intrusion not easily soothed with ointment, placated with an ice-cream frappe, nor escaped by feigning a need to pee. In the quiet of the walk, my chattering antagonists show their might now that I am no longer shielded behind busy family responsibilities, work schedules, or household priorities. They particularly like to play ping pong with my inner critic:

"You're not smart enough."

"I am!"

"Your voice is weak."

"It's not!"

"You are fooling yourself."

"I might be."

Everybody's journey has a beginning. Mine commences decades before the start of the Happiness Walk.

I hit the ground running in the back seat of a 1957 Ford station wagon wandering around Massachusetts looking for UFOs, my mother's preferred family pastime. There were a lot of reported sightings in the early sixties, and my mother wasn't going to miss out should one want to beam her up.

Mom was a vibrant, steal-the-show, let's-play-a-game kind of person. She was not only the life of the party—Joyce *was* the party. And she was one of the most generous and kind-hearted people I've ever known.

Mom suffered from chronic depression, the kind of bankrupted anima that causes one to believe death is a better option than life.

I remember my father waking me and my siblings to take us on a scouting trip to look for my wandering Mom one moonless, winter evening. Someone found her—luckily not us. I wouldn't want that haunting memory. There were plenty of others. She had plunged into the icy waters of Lake Quinsigamond in Worcester, Massachusetts, not far from where we lived. Though an excellent swimmer, she did not swim. That night led to yet another lengthy hospitalization at a time when therapy equaled fistfuls of Valium, incessant electric shock treatments, and bars on institutional windows. My mother had her own army of saboteurs, and they weren't as playful as mine.

It's possible that is how some people remember my mother. "Poor Joyce. She had a tough life." And she did. Her secrets were buried so deep they were never quite exhumed. She masqueraded her pain with drink and dance and laughter and, what I learned more recently, men.

Much too early in her life at an age not much older than I am now, my mother was drafted into the bleak and foggy world of Alzheimer's disease, then not much understood. She regressed slowly at first, so slowly in fact, that we, her family, didn't recognize it. "Oh, that's just Mom," one of us would say when she got stranded at the Hunan Garden restaurant without money to pay her bill or when she called the police to report her upstairs neighbor was stealing her underwear.

But it could not be denied when we learned a predator had escorted her to the bank to withdraw the amount of her monthly Social Security check nor when vodka became her favorite breakfast food. It wasn't because of the alcohol nor typical memory loss due to aging nor artistic eccentricities nor "just Joyce" we witnessed. We were losing our Mom.

I received many gifts from my mother, two of which are my love of dance and painting. Regrettably, neither play an active role at the moment in my life. However, a great life lesson she artfully modeled, one I reflect upon almost daily, is to "know that you don't know." Mom recognized that we all camouflage ourselves to masque our blemishes and bruises. She knew that the wholeness of who we are is rarely what we project onto life's movie screen, that we are so much more than the behaviors we assume or the roles we adopt.

Mom's compassion far outweighed her frailties, and her generosity crossed the threshold of every marginalized person she met. Her empathy and wisdom sprang from a deep well of knowing tapped into at a young age as she struggled to make sense of her abusive, abstract world.

Joyce earned everything she had the hard way. She lost it that way, too.

Even after she could no longer put a sentence together nor use a fork to feed herself, she imparted another life lesson. Mom taught me the powerful meaning of presence. Unlike many people with that plundering disease, Joyce was a happy camper. She sang with the birds, joked with the staff in her eventual residential care facility, and even fell in love with my father again: a source of great amusement within the family. She would laugh at the same joke over and over, sing the same song over and over, give the same compliment over and over, and tell me she loved me over and over and over again. She was the personification of presence . . . just here and here again, with a total moment-to-moment consciousness of now.

"Every moment is where we all have everything," said Andrew. I met him during his three-year walkabout on a rather busy street one hundred miles south of Mobile, Alabama. As a veteran, he was on a mission to keep each moment simple. "If you don't have anything in the moment," he continued, "then you're just thinking too far back or too far forward." Since Mom couldn't think in either direction, she was in the exact right place all the time.

"Maybe the journey isn't so much about becoming anything," I once read. "Maybe it's unbecoming everything that isn't you so you can be who you were meant to be in the first place." I think that's what Alzheimer's did for my mother. It removed her cloak and revealed her stripped-down, unobscured, authentic self. In the end, she finally got the peace she didn't even realize she deserved. I hope somewhere deep down in the waning flame of her spirit, she felt the serenity that visited upon her.

Mom would have loved this walk. More accurately, Mom loves this walk: I swear she has been with me from its start. As we placed her to rest in June of 2011, a single dragonfly lit on her ashes where it remained until her family exhausted all of our stories of our beautiful, eccentric, playful, compassionate, and loving Joyce.

Twelve months later, dragonflies guide the Happiness Walk from state to state. They are so commonplace that whenever one shows up, whoever happens to be walking with me at the time and I casually call out "Hello, Joyce!" and she flits on ahead, showing us the way.

According to legend, dragonflies symbolize transitions. How appropriate that they would accompany me on my transitory adventure. How evermore appropriate my mother would choose such a beautiful, colorful, and winged creature to embody. Dragonflies are our reminders to break away from constrictions of what we think we know and to embrace what is yet to be known. If we are accepting, dragonflies will flitter their way right through our strongly held illusions and direct us towards pathways of fearless change.

Like Mom, I am a warrior. I am, if nothing else, tenacious (some would say stubborn), a quality one requires when accosted by menacing adversaries of the mind, some that threaten your sanctity. The battle of the warrior, as described in the *Book of Runes,* is always with the self. Wherever you go—there you are. There is no walking away any number of miles from the very thing that endangers you most. Mom knew that. And I know there is no dodging the urgency to dig deep inside, ferret out the nasty thought buggers and look at them in the light of day. It's terrifying, but it must be done, and to do it, I must cultivate dragonfly's aptitude for fearlessness.

I used to think life should be all peace, love, and light. And I believe someday it will be. I truly do. However, I've come to understand—and it took me thousands of miles to get here— that darkness is an undeniable part of the intelligent design. We cannot see the stars without it. Why on Earth, quite literally, would we have free will if we were not expected to confront the ugliest parts of ourselves and, by doing so, reach for the stars? Or the alternative, acquiesce—and I refuse to surrender to anything other than light. So I became a warrior—not in an angry, fighting-against-an-enemy sense but most definitely in the torch-wielding, freedom-seeking, sovereign-soul-loving that's-so-like-Joyce way.

Best to be familiar with your aggressors than to have them shrouded in mystery, so I give thanks to the distortions of my mind for flagrantly revealing themselves. I say thank you for their tactical advancements, for staking their flags in the ground of doubt and fear, and for drawing me out into the open field of vulnerability to see clearly what I am made of.

Only I give them form. Only I clad them in sheaths of armor. Only I fortify their troops by conceding any moment of my attention. And conversely, only I can unclench their grip by refusing to be a pawn in their playbook. Then I see that they are me.

We each have the power to magnetize our minds to our advantage, points out the Reverend Mac Legerton of Pembroke, North Carolina. Mac is allergic to colloquialisms. Every one of his eloquent phrases subdues the monkeys in my mind as he preaches to my heart and not my head.

Long before I am regaled by the beauty of the western deserts, Mac and I chat over eggs and coffee at the Huddle House in a North Carolinian county where one-third of the population lives in poverty. Mac has taken me and my walking partners under his wings this week, providing lodging, events, transportation, and most generously, his wisdom.

Mac gifts me a ten-inch green wooden placard with large white block letters that now sits on a bedroom windowsill: "Make up your mind *and* be happy." He crosses out the word *and* and inserts the word to: make up your mind to be happy. He explains how our minds are the choice makers and creators of our felt experiences and how, by freeing our minds, we may choose to feel happiness rising in us. That is an important distinction from happiness achieved through battle. Honestly, fighting against anything is simply too energetically fatiguing. Rather, using the ancient Hawaiian healing practice of Ho'oponopono, a disarming expression of gratitude sends adversaries into retreat: "I'm sorry, please forgive me, I love you, and thank you." So, I must go about my business to create my own happiness.

As years pass, walking teaches me to not pursue anything, to be victorious in my own world of creation. It is a long road with many diversions. I'm too stubborn and too set on autopilot to observe earlier signposts. I bypass so much of life's beauty while I wallow in fear and in notions of victimization as I often forgo all the potential around and within me.

I have regularly consulted Angel Cards these past years. The one that continues to surface is Surrender. After much practice and years of cultivating an attitude of detachment, I surrender to simply being who I am—as best I understand who I am—on this rotating orb of a planet, within this endless universe, to allow life to unfold in all its splendor. I now know I am ready to surrender into the warrior within me.

So I set off to free myself from the onslaught of negative thinking. I engage my allies and deploy wisdom to the front lines instead of bullets of anger, sarcasm, and blame, my go-to defenses. I have simply found a lighter and happier way of being where free will replaces force and dragonflies replace monkeys.

Merlin cautions that "whenever a man tells a lie, he kills a part of the world." I realize that I have innocently lied to myself for years, and, by that, I've lied to others. I have a lot of restitution to make and a self-imposed prison to escape.

Just as walls restrict movement outward, they also protect us from dangerous forces beyond. Now, without prison bars to qualify the content of my life, all manner of newness creeps in. It is life-affirming, and I boldly move through the years with more energy, focus, and joy. At times, though, that exposure invites more than I bargain for, as is my experience in the desert of New Mexico when I unknowingly summon the interest of a mountain lion.

photo by Nancy Coons

Paula carries a new red umbrella into the rain.
The umbrella later succumbed to a snowstorm in Utah.
Paula leaves the home of her Brookings, Oregon, host on
April 4, 2018 at 5,526 miles during
Leg 13 of the Happiness Walk.

A RED UMBRELLA

It takes time, but we can do something every day to change the world, to push it in the right direction. People may think very differently, but that doesn't mean they disagree strongly. We just have to hear one another.

-Robert Beezat
Mount Pleasant, Michigan

Like a turtle, I walk slowly and with resolve, protected by the strong shell of a body I've honed. Turtles are teachers for walking your path in the flow of life just as they flow effortlessly through water. Though dragonflies never left the walk, I receive the blessings of many other animals throughout the years. Each leg of the walk procures a corresponding animal totem. I don't choose them - they choose me. Among them, I am guided by horses, grasshoppers, owls, salmon, snails, and a mountain lion. Each animal brings me wisdom and protection needed for the moment. But it is not surprising the turtle becomes the totem and guide for the full length of the Happiness Walk.

May 16, 2016
32.2329°N, 104.9000°W
Ramon, New Mexico

In the silent, desolate corridors connecting cities to hamlets to farms to forests, my three-mile-per-hour pace brings me

39

to a lonely desert byway towards the Turquoise Trail in New Mexico. I am alone but for the antelope and cattle that dot the landscape. An occasional jack rabbit skirts through the walking stick cacti, and prairie dogs leap to attention to warn their coterie of my approach.

Everything out here pokes, bites, or stings. Road signs forewarn of rattlesnakes, so I flinch with every rustle of the low, brown grass. I'm wary of venturing off the quiet road to relieve myself, so I mark the pavement along my way as a dog marks its territory. Because rattlers avoid the full heat of the sun, they are less worrisome when I stick to the asphalt during the day. But I'm on high alert towards dusk and am right to be so. Though they are as reserved as I when they appear, I guardedly abdicate my ground and veer around them.

My quietude eventually invites the companionship of a mountain lion. I catch her movement to my left and dare not change my stride. I reduce my motion to the essential. We timidly measure our footing, one with the other. Her tracks parallel my trail. We steal benign glances—a noticing. My heartbeat remains as constant as my gait, my feet barely touching the ground. Grace expands each fractal of space. I softly whisper, "Hello beautiful." Ears perk. I give more, "Thank you for walking with me." We respectfully acknowledge the convergence of our travels, my two-legged and her four-legged passage on Earth. We saunter in tandem until her curiosity is satisfied. I am sad to see her shift towards the horizon. She never looks back to say goodbye.

I am overcome with awe—spellbound. Shivers surface on my arms underneath my all-season jacket. Its only after I am left alone that I dare stop. I wrap my arms and hug the moment into my memory—never to forget.

Such is the fleeting nature of many encounters on the road. People move quickly in and out of my life yet leave a lasting and powerful impression. As with the mountain lion, I want to know them on a more intimate level, but the road calls. I take photos, share hugs, and never forget. Unavoidably, I miss capturing a photo of the lion when I recognize the motion is not essential. Much more importantly, the scene is indelibly imprinted in my memory—as are images of all the people I meet.

I was introduced to the world of mysticism early in my years. My explorations led me to discover the spiritual nature and ancient symbolism of animals. I consult my Medicine Cards and affirm the significance of my encounter. Mountain lion medicine is difficult medicine, I read. It involves lessons of leadership and calls for strong conviction, balance, and truth telling. If that energy comes to you, you are counseled to "lead yourself where your heart takes you . . . lead without insisting others follow."

Until I fully embrace the wisdom-quality of my intuition, Medicine Cards, runes, crystals, dowsers, and Angel Cards are my metaphysical training wheels, and they rarely fail me. When I meet Mountain Lion, I am still grasping on to my marriage, ruminating about how things got to where they were and how to salvage a friendship from all the hurt.

Neither Jeff nor I want a divorce, but we both know it is the right avenue for us. Believing it is the honorable thing to do, we wait for the kids to grow up. Even in my underlying discontent, I'm convinced I could stay—I have been conditioned for such a long time into sacrificing my needs and stifling my desires. Perhaps Jeff would say the same of him. We make a plan, but the pull of inaction proves easier.

Much like my mother and the awful disease that took her, we said goodbye to our marriage long before its actual death.

As with many couples, I see now that we simply grew apart. Unfortunately, our friendship atrophies at the same rate as our marriage. We coexist in that state of homeostasis for far too long until I am finally shocked out of paralysis. Everything that subsequently transpires shouldn't matter, but for some reason, I don't fully embrace that view until years later.

It's a wonder my legs withstand the weight of my agony. As I make miles under my feet, the "whys," the "hows," the "whos," and the "what ifs" are all new ping pong volleys for my monkeys until the parasite of "when" replaces them. I need to see the order of things. I need to know when my life was real and when it wasn't, when I began deceiving myself and when I began believing the deceit to be true—when Jeff whispered what I could not hear before he was obliged to show me.

The final push towards divorce induces the first thrust of birthing my new life. It is painful and at times insufferable. The cut leaves scars, but the result is freedom. The crowning achievement is me finding me.

Thank you, my feline self purrs. I'm following the road where my heart takes me, and no one needs to follow. I walk on my own with conviction as well as with the understanding that I am not truly alone.

I have just left the heaviness of Roswell. It is one of the few places where I still tap into loneliness and from where, including the entire state of Nebraska, I am eager to move on. I find it disappointing, because Roswell is one of the cities I was most eager to visit, having been raised on alien-scouting and all. My mother would have been disappointed, too, except for the International UFO Museum, which I don't take the time to visit. I miss a lot of the touristy stuff wherever I go, but I make up for it with the uniqueness of what others typically miss by walking past sewerage and wastewater management, recycling centers, and sanitation departments where the grime and the grind knead the operational yeasts into the underbelly of a city.

There's nothing comfortable about Roswell. I continue to conduct lengthy interviews, but I make few warm or honest connections. I feel estranged, but my schedule and spreadsheets keep pulling me back here to the Mozzarella Cheese Capital of the World, because there is nothing ahead of me for ninety-eight miles.

I always have a solid strategy for how far I intend to walk and which towns I plan to stop in on any given day. I love a good spreadsheet. I spend hours researching the safest routes, places of interest, resources for food and lodging, and people with whom I hope to connect. Always balancing my mission to promote GNHUSA goals with a need for forward motion, I contact as many media outlets and plan as many events as reasonable before I set out. If I stay in one place too long, I forgo connections made for the towns ahead.

The basic ingredients don't change. My notes are seventeen columns wide with rows as numerous as the days planned for each leg of the walk. There are hours of sunlight, terrain, and snakes and mountain lions to consider, all of which determine how much headway I can make on any given day. Add another walker to the mix, and everything changes: the pace slows, miles are reduced, hotels replace tenting, and bathrooms take precedence over bushes. As each leg of the walk begins, the Excel sheet represents more of a hope than a blueprint.

I am already ahead of my schedule but choose nevertheless to advance to Santa Fe rather than spend more time in Roswell, as much as I love cheese. Besides, my turtle-shelled body is now more at home in the desert than in this city.

I've been on the road for forty days on the current leg of
the walk prepared for the sixty-degree weather I met in Texas
but less so for the forty-degree days a month and a half later,
some of which has to do with the elevation. As usual, I make
do with layers.

I enter New Mexico from Texas by descending a thousand feet
from the Caprock Escarpment forty-seven miles east of Roswell.
I don't realize how striking the transitional landmass dominates
the scene until I turn around. I liken it to the Grand Canyon
without the canyon but with the stunning muted crimson and
ochre colors that blaze florescent mirroring the setting sun. To
the west is straight road with sage brush and dust. Even the
prickly pear cacti don't care to call that stretch their home.

It's still a two-day walk into Roswell. I'm excited to get there
but I've already walked twenty-six miles. I'm contemplating my
next move when an old van with Infowars and US Marine Corps
stickers makes a U-turn and pulls to my side. The driver offers
up a plastic milk jug with a brownish liquid, which he tells me is
water. I politely refuse. "Here," he says. "Have a beer instead."

Though it sits on his front seat in the glare of the sun, I take
it. Carbs, I reason.

Using the opportunity for an interview, I agree to sit on the
bumper of his old van. As he swings open the back doors, an axe
falls to the ground. Oh boy, be careful here! He recedes far into
the van and emerges with an Oscar Schmidt guitar. Bobby wants
to serenade me. And, hoping the innocence I see in him is real, I
allow it.

Plus, carbs!

He sings his favorite song, "Behind Blue Eyes" by Pete
Townshend. Unsurprisingly, he is a lonely man who wants

nothing more than to have "a girl my size," on the back of his motorcycle, and when we meet again later, he suggests I might be that girl. I am, however, definitively not.

So that's how I come to know him—Bobby Wants a Girl, a sad man behind blue eyes. Startlingly, he is quite talented, and I enjoy the seventies music he strums until he finally proposes to drive me into the city. I await an offer before I am reduced to asking. I rarely ask.

"I have a lot more songs."

"Yeah, but I have a lot of walking ahead, and it's getting late."

I learned the art of innuendo from my mother.

"Do you want a ride instead?" is his sympathetic reply.

"Well, sure. If you don't mind, I'd appreciate that."

I spend several expensive nights at El Rancho Palachio before Barbara Scheer offers five days hosting at Villa Park Senior Manufactured Housing. As I do not resonate strongly with its people, it is difficult to find a host in Roswell, but a side trip to a bird sanctuary along my route guides me to Barbara. She assures me that I do not sit alone with my feelings of alienation. She, too, finds it a challenge to build community in this place.

Bobby and I continue to meet up as he becomes my support person for 140 miles as he brings me to and from my starting points on the back of his Harley. Ironically, I become a girl on his bike for a short spit of time, but not in the way he fancies. The last day we see one another, we have breakfast at Denny's. Bobby is in a brown World War II military jacket covered with patches, pins, and medals, none of which he earned, some of which were his grandfather's. On the back he has pinned an American flag and underneath his coat is a tie-dye t-shirt. He hands me a gift. Bobby has put together an album of his life in old family photos, rudimentary drawings, and random text for me to carry the memory of him. The axe, his daily drive-bys, his anger at the world, that he is a Teutonic Knight, and the notion that at age sixty-four he lives with his mother somehow don't disturb me. This offering does.

I don't fully understand the meaning of his gift-giving gesture. He may be pouring his whole heart and soul into a relationship of his imagining, he may be innocently expressing himself in an adolescent manner, or—and I shudder to think of it—he's divesting himself of his worldly belongings to a kind stranger because he won't need them any longer. Whatever way, it unsettles me.

Bobby drops me at yet another hotel in Vaughn. Before he leaves, he favors me with a "friends forever" pink pendant and an Iron Cross ring then says with bluster, "I don't apologize for being white."

He tucks his shoulder-length, thinning white hair under his German helmet and rides the rattlesnake byway back to his mother's for his afternoon nap.

It becomes evident during our minimal time together that Bobby sees me as a possible girlfriend. It has happened a time or two on the road even though my neon sign clearly flashes "off limits." A romantic relationship is not what I seek nor am I capable of having at the moment. I hope when the walk is over I can open myself to that possibility, but today I cannot fathom it. I keep my sign flashing and wish it were easier to have interactions with men without their overlay of desire. So when I get to Vaughn, I am happy to leave that foolishness behind as well as all the other layers of heaviness in Roswell.

From my newest home base, I will make miles on foot for a couple of days by retracing the route I rode on the back of a motorcycle. On one of those days, I will meet a mountain lion. I am markedly happy to be distanced from the city and steeped in the desert.

I need the hotel in Vaughn because there aren't many people around to host me, though expenses dwindle my bank account as fundraising drips along in occasional five- and twenty-dollar increments. I'm not yet tenting. It isn't until up the road in Santa Fe, 3,456 miles into the project, that I am fully outfitted for the expedition, thanks to Biker Chic Nic. That is how she introduces herself in the City of Holy Faith, and therefore that is how she's affectionately christened in my phone contacts.

Nic Blouin helps me acquire camping equipment that allows me immense freedom and flexibility with choosing destinations. I stuff my new tent, tarps, stakes, poles, and sleeping bag into my youth-sized backpack that adjusts to my small frame. To make my new gear fit, I remove anything nonessential, including deodorant, curling iron (what was I thinking?), and my good bra. In my last attempt to save ounces I break my toothbrush in half and remove cardboard from the toilet paper roll. And even though they result in more bulk, I keep a steel carabiner coffee cup with instant coffee, a printed copy of my spreadsheet and a red umbrella for the rains yet to come—all adding up to twenty-eight pounds.

I benefit further from Nic's vast long-distance cycling, as she introduces me to Warm Showers, a hosting website for bicyclists, and teaches me about the generosity of many fire stations. The Happiness Walk is never the same after I meet Nic. I'm able to travel further from highways and into the most rural areas of our country, even though they are hard to avoid. Nevertheless, I'm certain I wouldn't have camped out anywhere with rattlers and mountain lions.

Plan, plan, plan, then let life happen is my motto.

After Santa Fe, I am ready for anything. I no longer require a town with a motel should a host not materialize. Rather I coddiwomple my way around the states—still traveling in a purposeful manner but with vague destinations. I can rest wherever my twenty-nine-square-foot MSR Hubba Hubba can fit as long as there is food and water close by: behind churches, in park pavilions, next to municipal pools, under store porticoes, in shelters for barbecue pits, and thanks to Nic's advice, on multiple patches of lawn at fire stations.

Still, camping is a second-to-last resort, right before moteling it. My goal is to meet and interview as many people as reasonable, so my hope is always to find a host with whom to dialog and a warm bed in which to sleep. This happens with great regularity and I am more than thrilled to abandon a twenty-eight-degree sleepless night in my bedroll no matter what its guaranteed temperature rating.

Such is the case three years later in Roosevelt, Utah—and four days into snow.

May 20, 2019
40.5070°N, 111.4133°W
Heber City, Utah

Customarily, I would be celebrating my thirtieth wedding anniversary on May 20 if the dissolution of my marriage hadn't been cemented two years ago soon after another noteworthy marker—dipping my toes into the Pacific Ocean. Instead, I find myself facing the imposing Rockies—ironic: timing is everything. Back in Massachusetts, my sister Chris pulls a daily Angel Card for me. Today mine reads as a prophecy—expansiveness!

I started the sixteenth and longest leg of the walk in Salt Lake City and have been on the road for only five days. Warm Showers hosts take me in as readily as a fellow cyclist. I have four of them lined up before I start, then I stay with a friend of a new friend before I reach an ascending road from the base of the Uinta Mountain Range. I am apprehensive about crossing the Rockies but talk myself into a decent, perhaps bloated sense of self. You need a good dose of chutzpah to do this walk. I also built in extra time for a slower pace allowing for frequent stops and shorter walking hours. The days are cold and snow hits before the week ends. My third red umbrella finally tears under the weight of soggy flakes.

Anyone who is the tiniest bit familiar with me knows how much I despise the cold. And I always am—cold. That is, I never take a trip without a pair of gloves even when walking the South in the summertime. So I've got an extra layer of grit I'm carrying along with my winter wear. I wear thick, cushioned Darn Tough Socks spun down the street from my once-Vermont home, a warm Skida Alpine hat emblazoned with the Happiness Walk's trademark (a gift also made in Vermont), a multi-use scarf, long underwear, and a lot of Chapstick. They're all part of the weight I carry.

I peek out from under my collapsed umbrella to see a car stop up ahead. I politely refuse the ride offered by Mr. and Mrs. Crosland and march on. I expect I look pretty outlandish walking in that sideways-spewing, blinding snowstorm.

Thirty minutes later, another car approaches. Out pops a ray of sunshine named Kristie who is on a five-hour drive with her husband, Marlin, to a Salt Lake City medical center for her "regular treatments," she tells me. Gregarious and forthright, within a few short minutes, Kristie Michaelson invites me to dinner when I reach her hometown in Roosevelt. That I heartedly accept.

As soon as they pass on, the Croslands stop again but from the opposite direction, this time bearing gifts: a bag of snacks, water, and a doughnut! I am a sucker for those delicious round morsels of goodness and could easily have named the walk In Search of the Best Doughnut. I didn't know it at the time, because my ruthless search is ongoing, that I already found the best one a year and a half ago when I walked through San Rafael, California. It was an unsuspecting vegan pastry from

Johnny Doughnuts, made with roasted sweet potatoes slathered with a light glaze and served with rich fair-trade, organic, black coffee. Perfection!

I walk the next hour to the Big G Café on US 40 in Fruitland. For the past twenty-eight miles, the only traces of habitation in the area are two closed campgrounds and an empty church. I use the stop at the café as an opportunity to stock up on a few items even though my notes indicate the next town of Duchesne has an Extended Stay Hotel, a sure sign of civilization ahead. I disrobe down to what is presentable and, around a six-top table, hang my soaking items to puddle on the floor. Adding hot soup and coffee to the mix, I nibble at my cruller and stow away the rest of the gifted snacks for inevitable desolate roads to my east as I make my way to Boston. For calories' sake, I force myself to eat. I am uncharacteristically not hungry. In part, my lack of appetite is connected to the fairly steady elevation of five thousand feet, down from eight thousand a few days before.

Uncertain of terrain I might encounter, I chose hiking boots for this leg of the walk rather than my tried-and-true running shoes. It turns out I was misguided. The boots agitate an old ankle injury and the weather doesn't help either: the stiff wet boots rub against my ankle causing blisters. I attempt a remedy by stuffing napkins inside my Merrells, causing my blisters to travel down to my heel and then toes. I wend my way with some level of discomfort until I reach Denver four hundred miles away where I feverishly scour the city for my favored Brooks Ghost Running Shoe . . . and my feet are happy once again.

My toes are still frozen but my nose warms up as I sit in the Big G Café. I notice the snowfall has mostly subsided as it floats like cotton from heaven, so I squeeze back into my not quite dehydrated garments and step back out into it. As I head east with vision restored, I am allowed to take in the view of a lake and canyons below to my right and a spray of red buttes to my left. I love the way the snow falls against Utah's red rock and how the resilient brush and blooms of the high desert pop their colors through the white canvas of snow. I love how the air is crisp and cleansing.

I love that there will be a shoe store in Denver.

A police officer promptly stops to check on my safety on one of the friendliest stretches of road I've encountered in a long while. And the neighborliness continues as the officer relays my whereabouts to two other officers, both of whom chaperone my sojourn, one waving me on from multiple checkpoints throughout the rest of his territory and the other packing me into the back seat of his cruiser to transport me to my evening's lodging. Tonight, in the snow, it's choice number three—a hotel.

By now I am conditioned to the bars and partitions between cruiser seats, the absence of passenger door handles and window controls, and truly uncomfortable, cramped plastic seats. But I am grateful for the generous rides from police and correctional officers all around the country and, as a result, have had many great interviews and conversations through metal cages. Once, near Snoqualmie, Washington, a police cruiser held me captive for an hour while the officer responded to an emergency call. Though I could have walked to my destination in the time it took to drive me there, I was warm and—now you know—that matters mightily.

Trucks rumble past as they carry their cargoes of oil and gas extracted from the sedimentary rock of the Uinta Basin. It is not a coincidence that the geologic depression sits just a hundred miles west of the Dinosaur National Monument where an abundance of dinosaur fossils date back 150 million years to the Jurassic Period. It makes me feel small and insignificant to contemplate the layers of history I'm treading in this vast expanse of natural—and captive—deposits.

Once the home of the Allosaurus, it is now Ute land. After forced government relocations, Indians' conflicts with the Spanish and Mormons, and tribal consolidations, the United States established the Uintah and Ouray Reservation in 1882. Consisting of 4.5 million acres, it is the second largest Indian reservation in the US with slightly more than 2,000 members.

I learn as I travel. Knowing so little of the Utes, I pause at the Fort Duchesne monument dedicated to members of their tribe who served in the armed forces, some before they were recognized as citizens of the US. A prominent plaque at the memorial wall reads

> For us, warriors are not what you think of as warriors. The warrior is not someone who fights, because no one has the right to take another's life. The warrior, for us, is one who sacrifices himself for the good of others. His task is to take care of the elderly, the defenseless, those who cannot provide for themselves, and above all, the children, the future of humanity.

I know not whether I subconsciously recalled the feelings I sat with during that stopover, but eight months later, I tattoo a small warrior rune symbol on my left index finger. An arrow. In white—for peace. In weeks following, I will return to the walk with many more native reservations and indigenous homelands to cross, my warrior mind indelibly etched on my finger and in my steps.

But for the time being, I am thumbing a ride outside my hotel on a May morning in Duchesne, Utah, forty-five miles west of Roosevelt and my soon-to-be reunion with Kristie. I receive a lift to my starting point from a quiet mother and her young adult son out from their campsite searching for coffee. As I hear so often, she never picks up hitchhikers but makes an exception with me. I am curious as to why. I'm not sure that I would even stop for me, but I'm grateful.

I've become accustomed to thumbing after decades of abstinence. I rarely have difficulty getting picked up even though the culture has not shifted with my newfound level of comfort. I used to pull my thumb in to avoid truckers, but eventually even those rides are welcome if not entertaining. Just two hundred miles before, I got picked up by Captain Ed Buns, a once exotic dancer turned truck driver who hails from my childhood state of Massachusetts. He showed off some of his moves and offered me a lap dance before I shut him down just as I did drunken Bernie four years earlier in Florida. My conversation with Captain Buns easily turned from erotica to Jesus Christ, his savior.

Oh, man, people are so multidimensional!

I'm hitting my stride.

I reach Roosevelt, Utah, two days after Kristie and Marlin first found me under my collapsed umbrella. As planned, I call to inform her of my expected time of arrival. The next thing I know, a dark blue SUV covered in magnets of large yellow and black happy faces and multicolored flowers is racing at me in the breakdown lane. The horn is tooting, and music is blasting: an amusing and festive welcoming.

For such a petite woman, Kristie lives life large. She cherishes every moment and admits you into her world so you, too, can fully experience her life force. We eat homemade lemon sour cream pie, dance in her living room, share our life stories, and sing until nightfall. Oh, how Kristie sings. To pass the many hours to and from her treatments for an ailment that remains undisclosed, Kristie dons multiple ensembles with colorful wigs and belts out the latest hits loudly and beautifully to her mixed tapes.

She also stops for strangers on the side of the road. And though she didn't realize it at the time, she manifested our meeting. After watching my interview on the Hallmark channel's *Home and Family* program, she thought she'd like to meet the Happiness Walker. Serendipitously, she invited me into her home before knowing that walker and I are one in the same.

For each positive person you embrace, your happiness quotient increases nine percent, I once heard. I don't know how you would measure that, but someone did. If this is true, go get yourself a Kristie to add to your life. I'm sure he or she would double your happiness impact quotient as Kristie has mine.

Early the next morning, with the gift of a brand-new red umbrella that Kristie found in her closet, I move on—but not away—from a new friend. I find the Ute memorial just six miles east from Roosevelt, pause to breathe in the enormity of its history, then continue towards the rising sun.

The road also rises as the days pass. I will climb to an elevation of 11,307 feet before three weeks are up. In advance of that, I must cross the Continental Divide (again), soak in hot sulfur springs, pitch my tent in several clandestine locations, avoid curious bears, meet a slew of amazing people (some in trucks), and eat several more doughnuts.

At the end of a leg of a walk, my printed spreadsheet is nearly illegible with scribbled-in routes, cryptic notes, crossed out towns, phone numbers and email addresses, news events and media, recipes, and conditions weathered. At times, it's a puzzle to figure out where I've actually been. When I get back to my home computer, I type in the adjustments, calculate the miles, add Kristie, Biker Chic Nic, and Bobby Wants a Girl to my contact list, marvel at how much I've crammed into so few months, and wonder how I could ever top such a phenomenal experience.

Of course, I do. And my Turtle Totem makes certain the days flow as harmoniously and with as much ease as possible as I move slowly and resolutely on this Earthly plane. Though sometimes it is the simplest things that can trip me up.

It was in November 2014 when I maneuvered a grassy bank in North Carolina and buckled as an invisible hole swallowed my left foot. My ankle swelled as I attempted to walk off the hurt. One mile later, I knew I had done some serious damage. I limped for the next five miles until I anemically crashed onto a sidewalk. I couldn't deal with the pain any longer. Sobbing, I hobbled into the closest store and did what you should never do; I removed my shoe. My foot and ankle immediately bloated beyond the stretch of my sneaker. I taped the ankle as best as I could, took some Ibuprofen, and—using a stick found on the ground as a cane— hopped another five miles to my waiting host.

Still, fortune smiled upon me when six-foot-plus Tommy Vann pulled two used crutches from his closet and whittled them down to my five-foot, one-inch frame. Voila! I was able to swing the remaining forty-two miles to Raleigh with a tidbit of ease. Wooden crutches aren't necessarily built for long distances, though, so I later abandoned them in a gas station with the hope that someone could adopt them and give them the screws and rubber tips they so badly needed. I went back to hobbling toward the state capital from there on, happy knowing I had four months to recuperate before my planned return after the winter holidays for leg number five.

An ambush of that kind should not catch one off balance on such a walk. You adjust, you accommodate, you listen to your internal GPS and navigate according to the new terrain. Some mishaps may even make you stronger. And within the unexpected, extraordinary things may also happen—like Mountain Lion: off the charts and once in a lifetime magnificent!

The pitfalls that genuinely blindside me are the ones I'm not yet able to brace against. The universe continues to offer me opportunities to rehearse weathering such disturbances until

I can manage them with an acceptable level of wisdom. One internal cyclone shakes me to my core in Tate's Hell. It jettisons my orientation as completely and absolutely as the undeniable absence of nails on my big toes.

*Prior to hitchhiking his way to Florida,
Freddie enjoys his morning coffee at a
Columbus, Texas, gas station on
March 27, 2016 at 2,682 miles during
Leg 9 of the Happiness Walk.*

DON'T GO THERE

If the fear is real, okay, but ninety-nine percent of the time it's not. It's something we've conjured up in our mind or other people have collectively conjured up for us. You've got to feel it; if you don't, you're not human. But then you've got to walk through it. You don't have to let it stop you or minimize you.

-Cheryl Godbout
Boise, Idaho

"I'm not a rapist" is what Scooter says as he hangs out the passenger window of the rusty blue GTO adorned with a rusty spoiler and sputtering exhaust. "What you doin'? You need a ride?"

I am walking a back road towards the crossing of St. Mary's River from Kingsland, Georgia into Yulee, Florida. I don't slow down as Scooter continues to chat but he and his two companions, Quick and Teri, are persistent. They are not content to be waved along with assurances that I am intentionally walking and don't need a ride. It becomes clear they want to connect, so I finally stop in front of a boarded-up motel where grass is winning its battle with paved driveway. No one has been here in a while, but I'm scanning just the same for signs of life. I'm always aware of

59

my surroundings, not expecting things to go south but prepared for it just the same. Quick turns the engine off, and all three vacate the car, Teri shyly clinging to her husband.

"You goin' where? You ain't gonna walk to Jacksonville. Promise us. It dangerous, man. We drive you there." They plead with me to take their advice if not their ride.

Wherever I go, it is the next city or town that is not to be trusted. It is rare I am told "You don't want to be *here*," and even that I take with a grain of salt. What is to be feared is twenty miles down the road, the next town over, or across the river. It's *there* not *here* where violence, discord, and danger lay in wait, readied to stalk new prey.

I've walked in denigrated neighborhoods with barred doors and glassless windows, past vicious dogs chained in front yards of farmhouses, through towns where correctional facilities are the main industry, into tent cities, by methadone clinics, around people drugging and drinking on park benches, and even between two brawny men with handguns tucked in the waist of their pants as a drug deal got transacted. But for the people who live there, the danger is elsewhere. They know their turf and have carved out a sense of safety, or in the very least, familiarity. I do the same. The slice of sidewalk or the shoulder of the road where I am at any given time is my sanctuary. I am safe, aware, and protected. My turf travels with me.

"Aren't you afraid?" I am frequently asked.

"No," is my generic answer.

But sometimes, very infrequently, I am.

September 30, 2015
29.8835°N, 84.5957°W
Lanark Village, Florida

It is in Florida, but not Jacksonville, I find myself on another desolate road in Lanark Village with little to no traffic, just south of the Franklin Correctional Institution and bordering Tate's Hell State Forest.

Up ahead dressed all in black—long sleeves, trousers, and a full face covering on a hot summer's day, a man walks towards me. He ducks into thick woods before he pops out again. He acts erratically and carries a long stick.

He and I get closer.

Where are the cars when you need them?

To thwart his advance, I casually cross the street to give the illusion I am taking pictures of the beautiful Gulf, which I've just seen for the first time. Then I turn my camera in the direction of the assailant to let him know he is captured on camera should anyone find my phone after he hacks me up with—what I've now decided—is a machete.

He ducks into the woods again.

Still, no cars.

I hold my phone to my ear and feign a loud conversation with my sister. There is no cell coverage. Otherwise it would be a real call.

Perhaps he will be dissuaded from abducting me if he thinks someone knows my whereabouts, would detect his boot imprints, determine the boot style, then trace it to the exact store where they were purchased, thus identify the inscrutable owner.

He gets closer. He isn't looking my way, and I am trying not to stare in his direction.

Closer still.

I've been here before. That summer night as a young twenty-something. I'm jogging past my old high school. It's dusk. I'm caught off guard when a figure emerges from the shadows. He's short and stocky. I see the blade of a knife. His footing is unstable. His pants are unzipped. I hope to skirt around him and pivot left. He lurches and drags me into the dark bushes. I fight. I feel the blade and his skin against me. I squirm. He fumbles. I'm slashed as I break from his grip. My feet race, as does my heart. I am safe.

Am I safe?

I don't feel safe.

Then it becomes clear to me. The man I see up ahead, the man-in-black, is weed-whacking. He is clearing the thicket from the side of Route 98, the road with no traffic. He isn't looking at me at all. He isn't interested in me at all. He gives no indication he sees me—at all. His stride never halting, he drifts past on the opposite side of the street. He attacks the weeds and leaves me to reel in the wake of my own storm.

I know I am doing it while I'm doing it. My head is in the 1970s while my sneakers are in the Sunshine State. Though time travel helps me prepare for anything untoward that might happen, it also obscures what *is* happening. I am still acclimating to being on the road alone and have yet to trust myself fully. I allow the voices and visions in my head dictate my circumstance.

I don't claim my turf.

In the moment, there is a fine line between wielding caution, brandishing street smarts, and trusting things always will work out for the better. I know it is a lesson I must practice and that I'll continue to get whacked over the head until I master it. My chance to hone those skills comes as early as later the same day when I find myself walking in the dark with crafty bears and covert weed whackers strategizing my demise behind the wooded tree line and me with only a phone as a flashlight and moxie as a weapon.

I make a vow to myself, then and there, that I will never again walk alone in the dark.

March 27, 2016
29.7066°N, 96.5397°W
Columbus, Texas

Freddie is not a weed whacker, but I'm pretty sure weed factors into his daily lifestyle. He is drinking a cup of Burger King coffee at a picnic table outside a convenience store in Columbus, Texas, on a sunny March morning. Painted in ink up and down his exposed arms, with teardrops tatted below his right eye, Freddie holds a placard that reads "HOBO LOVE BISCUITS and BEER." The smile beneath his white beard and mustache warmly matches the smiling sun he drew on his well-traveled cardboard sign.

I learn quite a bit about Freddie's history over our second cup of tasteless coffee. He is hitching to Florida to see his son from whom he is estranged but with whom he hopes to reestablish a relationship. He isn't sure how he will be received, but he is willing to attempt a reconciliation.

It's one of those days when, after I put in twenty-six miles, I return to my room at the Columbus Comfort Inn. I am told I am very lucky to get it. I learn there is a week-long antique show in the area and hotels are booked a hundred miles in every direction. I don't want to take any chances of being stranded, so I hitch a ride back to my day's starting point, as I am not yet equipped to camp.

The warm day transitions into a cold and dreary evening. I meet Freddie once more sitting on the curb of a second convenience store, his packs on the pavement and his sign tucked away. Unsuccessful in hitching a ride out of Texas, he settled into a stale cup of coffee instead.

We share a freshly cooked burger and fries from my takeout bag, the anticipation of which I had been salivating over for ten miles before its purchase. I think it was the least I could do. It's Easter, after all.

Then I am moved to offer more.

Freddie's story is horrific, but unfortunately not as uncommon as I would like to imagine. It involves abuse and abandonment as a child, drugs soon after, guns at some point, knives still, homelessness as a habit, volatile love with hopes for the real deal, jail time in the distant past, and sometimes a beer or two. He tells his story. I listen. I hear a genuine, lost man with a very big heart talk about survival, hope, and family.

I've been informed tattoo teardrops are associated with prison culture. We've already established prison as part of Freddie's past. The teardrops can also indicate the number of people the person has murdered (Freddie has two teardrops) or the death of loved ones. What his symbolize, I never learn.

"What would you say if I offered you space on my hotel room floor tonight?" It had begun to drizzle, and I was already shivering, but I had the promise of warm refuge awaiting me. Freddie's shelter, he tells me, is on a plastic garbage bag near the dumpster in the alley behind the store. "Give me one hour," I say so I have privacy to wash the walk off me, "then I'll meet you in the lobby."

After my shower and forgoing my usual sleeping attire, I fully dress and arrange couch pillows on the floor to create a bed for Freddie. He is in the bathtub and has been there for an hour. Throughout, I overhear him mumbling to himself and grunting in what I deduce is gratification with creature comforts, things that until recently I took for granted. The water gets drained, then more water is drawn.

I sleep with one eye open and am startled to hear Freddie back in the tub at two in the morning. He takes three baths in all, and when he isn't soaking, he is resting on the hard wooden floor instead of the soft hotel cushions.

As predicted, he never tries anything untoward.

At the complimentary breakfast the following morning, he brashly complains to hotel staff that the free coffee isn't hot (it isn't) and the free buffet is subpar (it is).

I am confounded. That is something I would never do. My world of social graces and indoor voices is definitely not his. I know I'm walking around the country by myself, but I'm naturally pretty timid and acquiescent. Yet Freddie expects the hotel to live up to his standards even though his alternative was a dumpster and yesterday's bagels. So I find myself asking, *Why would I expect Freddie to lower his standards simply because his circumstances are not mine?* Then, I shock myself by asking, *Why am I so reluctant to ask for what I want?*

I am momentarily stunned, fascinated, embarrassed, and ashamed all at once.

I quickly realize I didn't offer anything to Freddie that wasn't freely given. This minute experience and those like it provide me a window into the world of others, and I try to learn from them all. Freddie is an example for me to speak up when I have a grievance, to smile at whomever passes, and to appreciate the value of a hot bath.

I'm pensive as Freddie and I depart to opposite ends of the country. He doesn't own a phone for me to check in on him, but he has my business card and calls from random numbers over the years. I learn his reunion didn't go as hoped, but he sticks around Florida for a while anyway. Eventually his calls stop, and I am left oblivious to the rest of his story. People come—people go.

As I hitch a ride back to Bastrop where I ended the day before to continue my way into Austin, my sense of "normal" feels a world away.

"I could never do what you do. I would be too scared," many say to me. But honestly, people aren't the real menaces of the road. Freddies and Scooters are not the danger. We have an unfortunate propensity to see one another as caricatures, and those we draw of people with whom we are unfamiliar are often foreboding and wholly distorted. I find that, when I dismiss all the biased conditioning of our culture, I am consistently greeted by people as a friend. Alone on the road, I find it most welcome. The friendships I collect are as the feathers and shells in my pocket: gems I treasure long after we first meet. I recall faces and specific places, but mostly the feelings are what fill up my memory jars.

Yet, I must admit to some danger on the road, and mostly the culprits are dogs. Just ask anyone who spends a lot of time on the streets. When I talk with other long-distance walkers or runners, cyclists or postal carriers, they promptly share their stories about run-ins with dogs.

Pit bulls. They are almost always pit bulls. My first encounter was in 2012 as I passed a remote, ramshackle Vermont farmhouse. An unleashed pit bull charged out from behind the barn and nipped at my legs. He broke skin on my calf, but I kept walking just fast enough to keep out of his reach and slow enough so as not to incite a chase. A few years and a few dog encounters later, I've taken to carrying mace, though thankfully I've never had to use it.

Now, I know some of you are fast dog lovers and will want to come quickly to their defense. Heck, Linda, my initial walking partner, is one of the most ardent dog lovers I know. Even so, the following story involves her.

Two years after the Happiness Walk began and with only
eight days of walking in 2013 into Montreal with my good
friend Skye Forest, Linda and I need to recondition our bodies
after deciding to take the walk across the country. It isn't until
later that we start talking about *around* the country.

Opting for a thirty-nine dollar Megabus ride from Vermont
rather than an expensive plane ticket, we arrive in DC to begin
where we left off at the Jefferson Memorial. Following an
emotional walk through Arlington National Cemetery, we hit
the busy streets of Alexandria, Virginia. It's rush hour, and the
traffic is bumper to bumper, but, in urban fashion, still fast. Out
from the back of a house bolt not one but two pit bulls headed
straight for Linda.

By then, both of us are well practiced on handling canine
encounters. We make ourselves look larger and bulkier than
we are. I often find a fallen limb (later, I will use my walking
stick) and sweep it in a large arc from one outstretched hand to
another. We employ low, stern voices directing dogs home, and
that's all it usually takes. Occasionally, a dog will simply want to
travel with us, so we must be more persistent and more stern.
But truly, most dogs I come across are wimpish and just want
affection. They usually achieve their goal, especially when Linda
is around.

You learn to sense potential danger with animals, though
some situations are more self-evident than others, like the time
just a few days later. It's hunting season as Linda and I take a
short cut along an old railroad bed. We startle two large dogs of
indeterminate breed, blood dripping from their growling mugs
as they safeguard a fresh deer kill. Slipping slowly and silently

backwards, we hide ourselves on the opposite side of the tracks, gladly conceding them their dining space.

But in Alexandria, the dogs do not succumb to our well-honed tactics. These are pit bulls and pit bulls are strong-willed, compact, muscular, and selectively bred for their jaw strength—a curious combination for a pet. I never approach one even though many owners swear they are the most gentle dog they ever had.

We must have caught those two unaware. As typical, we are on a non-pedestrian-friendly road. Linda and I cautiously make our way along the fringe without sidewalks or shoulders when one of the dogs charges down a bank right at Linda. Her reaction is frightening. She is clearly terrified, and her instinct is to back away from the assailing dog into the fast-moving, oncoming traffic.

Then comes dog number two.

I unsuccessfully attempt to engage that dog so it won't push Linda farther into death's door. Cars screech to a halt to create yet another layer of danger as fenders begin to tap. When the owner finally arrives, he has little control over his animals, which by then are exceedingly riled up. So is Linda. I don't want to appear hyperbolic, but if you can die from fright, I believed Linda's future was at risk—if not from the dogs, from the cars.

Fast-forwarding to the end of the story—Linda is fine; she is home safe in Vermont (I presume). Nothing terribly damaging came out of the situation (I presume), but it is certainly one I don't want to repeat (I know). Ever. Hence, the mace.

Linda, another co-founder of GNHUSA (there are four of us including Ginny and another Vermonter, Tom Barefoot), gave me strength to walk from the very beginning. She is the reason I am on this trip. What are the chances I would find someone in my hometown the very same age, with similar life views and life circumstances (grown children and, at the time, encouraging partners), with the same desire for a long walk and an audacious drive to change the world?

Linda and I were both state leaders involved in community-organizing work that stressed the prevention of social ills by building on "what works," pre-GNH-thinking. Heck, our eldest children even went to their high school prom together. It was all a sign! We had work to do together, it said. At the time, it wasn't clear what all that work might entail.

Over the first several legs of the Happiness Walk, gravity kept pulling Linda home but the elastic band that tied her to our mission kept snapping her back to the walk. Vermont would tug at her once again. Then she would recoil and land suddenly back on the road. As her comings and goings turned ever more unpredictable, Linda became both my survival and my albatross. I couldn't see through my ignorance back then, that those expanding moments in her absence were the fortuitous gift I needed to exercise my self-reliance, confidence, and independence to help me stand—and walk—on my own.

The elastic band predictably broke. After a full year of my mind encouraging me to move on and my heart chiding me for moving on, after twelve months of vacillating about what to do, I finally let my heart and mind agree. She's gone, I acknowledged, but more significantly, I'm on my own.

"Know that you don't know," Mom would say. I understand, though I didn't then, that what sometimes I characterize as good can easily turn into something not-so-good, and what I might label troubling oftentimes leads to better life outcomes. So, when things went south with Linda, I could anticipate that this too shall pass and something positive may very well come of it.

Indeed, that is what happened. But it took me way too long and many years for the monkeys in my mind to stop blaming and start owning my power.

"Let it go, let it go," repeat the song lyrics in *Frozen* that Ginny, who claims a young princess for a granddaughter, teaches me. She also informs me the song is less about releasing and more about letting your freak flag fly.

It appears I need to do both.

There would be protracted emails from Linda and abandoned plans made to rejoin in one state or another. Clearly, she remained in conflict for a while longer than I. I understand. She and I created the project together, and it can be unthinkable to abandon that which you love. Furthermore, there is definitely something bewitching about the walk that is hard to replicate off-road, which makes paving a life without it unimaginable.

Even people whom I've met briefly feel its draw. Scooter continues to call to make certain I am staying away from the bad sections of towns. Years later, Freddie checks in on me to update me on his travels until he goes silent. Others stay in touch via email, social media, cards and letters, calls, and gifts. Each person I've met enriches my life, and I hope the magic of the walk continues to touch their lives, as well.

I never found "the next town over," the one where I shouldn't travel. I never would have met most of the wonderful people I encountered had I not trusted my own discernment—had I allowed fear to usher me along the familiar, mainstream path or worse, paralyze me. Instead, with the nudge I received from Linda and later from my husband, I am moved to explore the dense overgrowth of life, not with a weed whacker but with a camera and recorder.

Of course, there are still circumstances that throw me off.

Every once in a while, I'll get a small stone in my shoe. My backpack cautions me not to bend over while, at the same time, my momentum begs me to forge on. Some days I hobble tens of miles with a pebble before I dispense of it. As in the old fairy tale, "The Princess and the Pea," the tiny interloper can despoil a day's gay walk. It can be devious; it moves, it hides, it disappears only to surface between my toes. It plays tricks on me, so I play tricks with it. I ignore it, I endure it, I diminish its existence in my mind. That is my tendency with the little things. When it comes to the big stuff, my approach gets more complicated.

Even through the bigger challenges of the walk, I discover what I never could have found in some mediocre caricature of a life that I might have allowed others to author. I learn to change my patterns and habits of thinking, strip away the falsehood of victimization, and begin to pen my own script. I wear my happiness pajamas on the outside as well as on the inside—during the day as well as the night. I let my freak flag fly.

Fellow wanderers understand the nature of freak flags. I reluctantly confide that Forrest Gump does, too, and that he and I share a lot in common, not the least of which is walking "through every kind of rain." Forrest appears instinctively to know what I have come to learn: happiness is a way of traveling, not about toeing the line or taking life in stride. It's a box of chocolates with a good cup of coffee.

Wearing only briefs, the Naked Cowboy takes a break from strumming his guitar in Times Square to answer Paula's questions on September 19, 2012 at 339 miles during Leg 1 of the Happiness Walk.

MRS. GUMP

Mama says they were magic shoes. They could take me anywhere.

—Forrest Gump
Savannah, Georgia

"Hey, you're a female Forrest Gump," people like to joke . . . a lot! Since its 1994 film debut, Forrest Gump has been designated a proper noun to figuratively suggest a simple-minded but good-hearted person involved by chance in historically significant events. I hope the many people who call me Mrs. Gump invoke this comparison based upon the number of miles on my shoes rather than the number they assign to my IQ. I don't ask.

Those folks might be on to something. It seems I've followed in Forrest's footsteps from New York City to South Carolina, all along the Gulf Coast, and as far west as the Santa Monica Pier. Embarrassingly, I even did the rare touristy thing and stepped into his bronzed shoes at Bubba Gump Shrimp Company restaurant in Times Square for a photo op. That was right after I interviewed—and was serenaded by—the very talented Naked Cowboy.

Perhaps not thinking I would comply, my best friend Cheryl Lopriore, who traveled to visit me for a few days in New York City, suggests I interview that Times Square icon. Apparently, she hasn't grasped the full meaning of seeking out the naked truth!

Cowboy boots, cowboy hat, white briefs, a guitar, and a smile are all the Naked Cowboy wears as he entertains hordes of passersby. He sings his answer to what matters in life and I blush while he strums his guitar: "I'm the Naked Cowboy keeping it real for you. Happiness is freedom and freedom requires courage—obviously, I sing and play in my underwear all day."

He ends with "Hey, don't forget your butt shot!" as he turns his torso and poses for the camera.

People and their antics rarely throw me off my game. And because I can come across as an oddity—someone walking around the country with a backpack—people often try. By the time I get to the South, not much can phase me except for dogs, of course, and yeah!—bears, boars, and cottonmouths.

Now, feel free to skip these next pages if, God forbid, you haven't seen the Forrest Gump movie or read the book. If that is the case, please put this book down and go read the acclaimed satirical novel. Come back when you can appreciate the following references.

Linda and I find ourselves by happenstance in Walterboro, South Carolina, the film location of Forrest's elementary school. Unlike Forrest, we have no intention of being in Walterboro. While only nineteen miles west of Charleston, on this particular day, Route 17 is the definition of a country road. It morphs in character from friend to foe as I wind my way down 360 miles from Myrtle Beach to Florida where the road and I finally part ways. Forrest, too, travels that road, though with a quicker pace than I. He has much longer legs!

We stop for grilled fried green tomato sandwiches and moon pies at the Harvest Moon Lowcountry Grille in Ravenel. Brad Kopsax, the owner, offers us a ride later in the day into Walterboro: a real town with lodging options, we hope. We walk another five hours before he picks us up. He's carting three bags of groceries and an assumption we will stay with him. So we do. He dishes up a five-star surf 'n turf dinner before we crash, Linda on his couch and me in a chair in the living room of his one-bedroom apartment.

The following night provides a contrast in accommodations but certainly not in hospitality. Linda has had a challenging couple of weeks. It is onerous for her to listen so intently to what people share without the requisite time to process, so we give ourselves a rare break and book a room at Hampton House Bed and Breakfast just two blocks down from Brad's apartment. Our innkeepers, Diane Forde and Henry Ruthinoski, thoughtfully organize two newspaper interviews and a cocktail party with four of their close friends, one of whom is Dargon. Remember her. I'll mention her again soon. So, while delightful, the stay isn't without its busy-ness.

The stage has been set. My walking partner for much of the journey to date decides to leave. She covers her last ground with me from Forrest Gump's school into beautiful downtown Beaufort. From then on, I am on my own, though encouraging others to join me as they can.

I'm disappointed and hurt. I feel betrayed—but of course that's my perspective. I gave up my employment, as Linda and I had each agreed we would, and rearranged my life around continuing a project to which I am decidedly committed. It took a toll on my marriage, but at the time my marriage seemed strong enough to allow for such risk.

Everything is changed.

I'm angry. I'm angry at Linda. I'm angry at Jeff. I'm angry at myself for being angry. And I'm angry for not being stronger and more compassionate. If you haven't guessed it already, I kinda like to finish what I set out to do—in every walk of my life, including personal relationships.

Of course, I can't expect anyone to be married to the same drives I have, but I truly thought I had enough in common with my walking partner to go the distance. I suppose I did, for a while, and so I eventually became grateful for the abbreviated path we shared.

I had an intuitive reading with Jean-Jacque Guyot from Quebec around the time that Linda left the walk. He knew nothing about me, not even my name. "Why aren't you walking?" he asked matter-of-factly. Even he knows me better than I know myself, I lamented. "Do not forget that you are the most important person in the world and that the best is yet to come."

I had forgotten. Actually, I never knew. And phew . . . it does get better!

Before Linda leaves, we have one more adventure. According to Forrest Gump trivia, Forrest's love interest, Jenny, grew up in a farmhouse on the Bluff Plantation near Yemassee, close to where we end our walk two days after surf 'n turf with Brad. In order to get back to our host one evening, we hitch a ride with a local mechanic in an old, rundown van that once was white but is now the color of rust. It is a chilling ride. Just like Jenny's father, the man has a love relationship with alcohol. It turns out our driver has no qualms about popping open a tall Budweiser or two while steering with his knees through the back roads along the Combahee River. Linda does a stellar job keeping him focused on the correct side of the road, but he has a penchant for passing four cars at a time. We both train our eyes on the center line and the beer, so we never do get to see the fabled farmhouse.

Bucolic Beaufort is where much of the award-winning film was made and one of the few places, thus far, I can see myself possibly calling home someday. It is historic and quaint with a vibrant downtown, has a great coffee shop (an absolute imperative), and is surrounded by water (an ambitious imperative). It even has a busy and friendly farmers' market. Most significantly, it is where I meet Joan, friend of Dargon's sister Peggy. Remember Dargon-friend to my host Diane? That's how it works.

When our new friends in Walterboro call Joan to ask if she could help me out for a night, she quickly replies, "Yes!" before Dargon can finish her sentence. I spend four amazing nights in the home of my newest host, though Linda's time is cut short.

Joan discloses how she surprised herself by inviting complete strangers into her home. "It just isn't like me. I've never done anything like this before."

I hear that from time to time. For some reason, people take a chance on me. It isn't as shocking to hear any longer. I've accepted it as one of the consequences of my persona as I wander about. I'm glad that I am the one people choose to take a risk on because I trust me, and I like to believe I am offering a pleasant and safe first experience. Perhaps my hosts will be more likely to stretch their comfort zones toward opening doors to newer ventures. I hope so, and in some cases, I'm told so.

About fifteen years my senior, Joan is a fit, petite woman with a Southern drawl that could melt the shell off a boiled peanut. Her hair is perfectly coiffed, her dress impeccable, and she is openly proud of her family, heritage, and her lovely town. A recent widow, Joan grapples with her first man crush after the husband she adored, so we talk about relationships. We also discuss health, history, children, art, and more, usually over a glass of wine and always over good Southern food. Luckily for me, I will see Joan twice more as I continue to make my way down the East Coast.

Among other sites, Joan takes me, Linda, and Carol Maloney, a mutual friend from Vermont who continues with me through Savannah, to the Beaufort Yacht and Sailing Club on Lady's Island. If it weren't an oyster-for-underwear fundraiser, we would have been terribly underdressed. The island provides the background set for much of the Forrest Gump movie, including Lady's Island bridge—in South Carolina, mind you—where, curiously, Forrest was welcomed into Mississippi. Lady's Island is also where the Bubba Gump shrimp boat was docked. In the movie, it was known as Bayou La Batre, Alabama. Ah . . . Hollywood! The funny thing is, I would later visit Bayou La Batre and meet Captain John who is an actual shrimper. His family, in fact, is an integral part of the bayou having settled there more than a hundred years ago.

October 29, 2015
30.5477°N, 88.1753°W
Theodore, Alabama

Captain John could easily have been a character in the Forrest Gump motion picture—any movie, really. Just before we met at my host Patti Edmundson's house in Theodore, Alabama, he shot a water moccasin right between the eyes with its mouth firmly clamped around a frog. It had slithered from beneath his front doorsteps. I guess that's what you do here in Alabama.

I fear water moccasins, also known as cottonmouths, most along the Gulf Coast—pit bulls, get in line. That's after I acclimate to the idea of nearby bears, wild boars, and alligators. I'm told the snakes are willful creatures: that they, unlike rattlers, will literally pursue you and jump at you from long distances, according to Alice Boudreaux, my host in Winnie, Texas, who was stalked in cotton fields and bitten . . . twice! I keep my eyes wide open, and, thankfully, the only encounters I have are with dead ones.

Captain John wears a well-earned gold anchor on a chain around his neck for all the hooks that have snared him over the years. He points to scars from multiple knife lacerations; the indent in his calf from a bullet shot through his leg during a scuffle; marbled, tattered skin covering his side from a motorcycle scrape with gravel, and a missing finger sawed off absentmindedly during a heated argument. His body has endured twenty heart attacks and received twenty stents. Partly because he's without medical insurance but equally calibrated to his demeanor, he often performs his own triage and stitches his lesions with a hook and fishing line.

The captain understands shrimping.

The captain understands survival.

He is a quiet and slight man frequently accompanied by an eight-inch wiry spiked-collared dog he playfully calls Killer. It is through his generosity that, two days later, I begin a free four-night stay in a fancy, cottonmouth-free casino in Biloxi, Mississippi, where I, like Freddie, appreciate the luxury of a bathtub.

Forrest would have enjoyed meeting Captain John as much as I did. My guess is he would also have fallen in love with Cindy, Christine, and Danielle. Oh, and most definitely, Christie.

April 23, 2015
32.0809°N, 81.0912°W
Savannah, Georgia

As I am home in Vermont making plans for an upcoming leg of the walk, I receive a call from California. Cindy Bair wonders if I would mind if she and her work partner, Christine Allen

Sloan, fly to Georgia to film a bit of the Happiness Walk and perhaps walk with me a bit.

Mind? It took us all of thirty minutes on the phone to become fast friends and make plans to meet at Chippewa Square: the bus stop in Savannah where Forrest shares his box of chocolates and narrates his life story. Cindy was the first of many to (somewhat annoyingly, but obviously correctly) make a tongue-in-cheek connection between me and the movie.

The ladies thought that square would be a good location to produce their online TV show, *Oh for the Love!*, a series about people doing interesting and unusual things with their lives. The Happiness Walk seems an unequivocal good fit. So, Cindy and Christine fly in from California and Utah, respectively, with Christine's daughter and camerawoman Danielle in tow. Cindy will later accompany me in Florida and again with one of her daughters, Lyndsey, in California. Three years later, I will also get to meet Christine's entire family when I stay with them in Lehi, Utah. Oh, for the love, indeed!

The bus stop is not on the square anymore, nor was it ever. I'm told a bus could not have made it around the corner at Chippewa Square, so traffic was reversed for a day. The bench, a movie prop, was strategically placed near Hull Street—cue in the chocolates and an iconic cinematic moment was captured in perpetuity. For tourists who play their cards right, a faux Forrest Gump can occasionally be seen running across the square, enjoying the attention he falsely draws. I'm not that guy. I'm rather camera shy, but with my good friend Christie Binzen, walking partner for the next hundred miles, I do my best to accommodate for the sake of the television show.

We film and laugh and cry together and listen to Christine perform an impeccably executed alligator mating call, a skill learned during one of *Oh for the Love!'s* recent episodes about alligator wrestlers. She turns alligators on their tails, and I, in turn, hide mine. Mercifully, there is a steep incline between meaty us and scaly them. Otherwise, Christine would find herself consorting with gators in ways she never dreamed possible.

October 7, 2012
38.9072°N, 77.0369°W
Washington, DC

There is also the time I stand in my walking shoes at the Jefferson Memorial in Washington, DC, where Forrest Gump receives his medal of honor. Now that is a sweet coincidence. The memorial is the deliberate destination of the very first leg of the Happiness Walk and where seminal instructions are indelibly etched into marble. President Jefferson advocated for a change in language within the Declaration of Independence from the words "Life, Liberty, and the Pursuit of Property" to "Life, Liberty, and the Pursuit of Happiness," a revision that has made a wealth of difference.

It most assuredly isn't property that manifests happiness. Stuff seduces generations of us Americans to live well beyond our means while exploiting the riches of the planet. Peter Ricca of Mount Vernon, New York, says it well, "Our society has made gods of money and position and eliminated the value of the human being."

Throughout the entire walk from NYC to DC to Savannah to Bayou La Batre to Santa Monica and back again, when answering the question as to what matters most, people frequently respond by declaring what doesn't matter. It may be easier for some to identify what they don't want before they discern what it is they do desire and value.

"Money. It isn't money." That's the spontaneous answer provided by an overwhelming number of interviewees like Vikram, whom I met in Orik, California, on an Easter morning over banana cream pie. He immediately responded that it's not the job or salary that gives him happiness. He would rather we pay attention to "making nice over making money."

"Momma always says," imparts Forrest as he sits on the bench munching confections in Chippewa Square, "there's only so much fortune a man needs and the rest is just for showing off."

I've sloughed off most of my material goods and parlayed them into a life of experiential abundance. I have enough money to be comfortable—it certainly plays a role in my life, but I haven't made it my raison d'etre, my reason to be. Like the thousands of individuals I interview intuitively understand, there's so much more that matters during our brief time on the planet than what is or is not in our bank accounts.

I confess that Forrest and I do have more in common than the places we share, after all. We both lead unrestricted lives, celebrate our core values, and love shrimp. Both of our mommas taught us that you may not get to choose which box of chocolates lands in your lap, but each bite of life can be a delicious surprise—so savor it!

"Momma always told me miracles happen every day. Some people say no, but they do," says Forrest.

Sometimes at the end of the day when my energy has waned and my legs are tired, I feel a force tenderly urging me along. It's not the wind. I'm certain of that. It's not nameable. It's like something that softly nudges the space at the small of my back, giving me no other choice but to keep moving forward one step at a time—odd, but welcomed. I've stopped questioning it and just accept it when it happens like so many wonderful and inexplicable phenomena on the road.

I've credited such aid to the work of my ever-present angel guide, but perhaps I'm wrong. Perhaps it is the spirit of Forrest

Gump who is gently pointing me home, its direction soon to prove complicated, since I will not have an address.

Paula, left, shares a laugh in 2015 with, from left, her father, Vern Johnson Jr. who, she says, was always good for a bad pun; her brother, Vern Johnson III, and her sister, Christine Johnson Noyes.

I SEE YOU

You can lead people and guide people in a direction . . . but the heart can only be activated by the self. You can have as many rules to help people activate that on their own, but ultimately it's up to us.

-Michael Durst
New Orleans, Louisiana

Now you know—I didn't start out this way, a solo walk within a solo life. Not long ago, I was a soccer mom and PTA member holding yard sales and neighborhood parties. I dutifully accompanied my husband to his national conferences in interesting boutique cities as I drank mimosas with the other wives, talking about our children's college choices, and vacations at his family's quintessential cottage on Cape Cod. My life had grown to be quite comfortable. It was safe and predictable with healthcare and a good retirement plan.

That life didn't come naturally to me. It's a far cry from what I once knew.

I grew up in a tight-knit neighborhood in a lower-middle class family in the town of Shrewsbury, Massachusetts, a bedroom town for Boston. We had mostly everything we needed, and when we did not, relatives and townspeople provided for us until we could manage for ourselves. Those moments debited my father's pride, though we children were largely protected from material deficits. With every passing year, our lot in life improved due to the efforts of my hardworking and thrifty father.

Dad was the first in his family to go to college, and I and my siblings were the first on my mother's side. Dad had an encouraging and nurturing family. Mom did not. Though in later years my father achieved the middle-American security he worked so hard for, my artistic mother never did. She subsisted on the yard sales she hosted and the paintings she could barter.

As a natural optimist, I have a nostalgic view of my childhood and am selective with my recollections. I remember family camping trips, hours of kick-the-can with neighborhood kids, and sipping coffee with my Aunt Carol in our yellow, sunlit kitchen. I fondly remember my starched first-day-of-school outfits hung on my bedroom doorknob, the stack of gifts under overly tinseled Christmas trees, and Grandma Kender's banana cream pies. I choose not to dwell on other childhood memories.

"It goes beyond survival when we automatically see the value of everything in relationship to the truth of ourself, our central self," says Michael Galligan, whom I met in Santa Fe. I know Michael's right. We must live in our truth, and to do that, we must know who we are, including our past as long as we don't allow it to define us or stunt our potential.

Michael speaks to the importance of looking beyond all the clutter in our lives, all the definitions of ourselves, all the ways we cast an image onto the world in order to uncover that esoteric something that makes us alive. When we do that, he suggests, we are able to see it in others. The insight often comes in the form of vulnerability.

When I meet her, Rashida Brooks is walking her bike with a flat tire on the Cape Fear Trail in Fayetteville, North Carolina. That moment leads to a new walking partner, several nights of hosting, family dinners, a neighborhood party, and keys to a car.

As friends and family finish their potluck meal on one of those evenings, I delve into my question around the dining room table. Because of the group size, people rotate in and out of one particular chair so they can more easily be recorded. This spot becomes known as "the crying chair." Tears frequently accompany interviews for a number of reasons—for losses interviewees feel, joys they experience, their pains, shames, loves, and sometimes for unknown causes. As observed in Antoine de St. Exupéry's The Little Prince, "It is a mysterious place, the land of tears."

Rashida's husband, Jack, takes his turn and guests hush or quietly leave the room. It is clear there's something everyone in the house knows and I am about to learn.

As with his predecessors, tears flow. They flow for several minutes before he's able to speak. We remain still. The room is dense with emotion, and several of us silently weep with him in the heaviness of that space. Jack's tears are steeped in pain and regret mixed with deep gratitude for his family and friends. His story is honest, poignant, unguarded, and, frankly, his business. But he honors his placement in the chair and divulges his repentant story of infidelity. Not fully understanding what prompts him to do so, I honor his candor.

Honestly, I have yet to meet a person who has not lamented choices they've made. Why they are revealed in my presence, I am unclear. Perhaps the baring of their souls frees them from whatever chains them to their painful story. I suspect people would be surprised at consistencies between the dramas of our lives, notwithstanding my own.

Jack reaches deep into the painful depths of his being to discover his central self. Through his guileless sharing and purging, all of us present become a part of his story, including a walker just passing through.

In like manner, eight months later in Florida, Ronnie weeps in his chair. He is confronting his own demons of racism. It's not news to say prejudices run like sludge in our American veins as they clog up our hearts and our minds. No matter our color, wealth, geography, or education, we must all inoculate against the malady that spawns the ugly condition. Confronting deep-seated beliefs takes courage and, for many of us, time. Ronnie is aware enough and vulnerable enough to expose himself to that truth—and he confesses his shame to me.

The Latin root of the word vulnerable is vulnus or wound. I believe that, when exposing someone else's wound, we become responsible for it. It may not astonish you to know that I feel quite responsible for many thousands of people scattered around this country. With trust as a backdrop, people can be incredibly candid. I am intensely grateful for the honor of being on the receiving end of peoples' stories; their trust in me is a validation of our human connection.

"The most important thing we can do is to see one another," says Ms. Claire, sitting behind a case of colorfully frosted cupcakes. Ms. Claire is the proprietor of the SilverSpoon Bakery in Portsmouth, Virginia. She abruptly excuses herself from our conversation and calls to a man passing by her shop. "Come meet me out back," she calls to him. "He's homeless," she explains, "He won't come in the front door, so I visit with him out back and give him some food. We talk, and he tells me things. I don't think he feels like people see him, but we all need that—it's basic to who we are."

I later meet a man in Austin, Texas. "Hello," I say in passing.

"Hello and thank you," replies Otis.

"Thank you for what?"

"For seeing me."

Otis is a WWII veteran. Though down on his own luck, he waits outside the social service office where he drove a friend who has no car. Otis is taking care of her needs. Immense sadness washes over me for being thanked for so little. To quote Gandhi, "The greatness of a nation can be judged by how it treats its weakest member." I'm disturbed to imagine what Otis's comment says about us.

Regina Amarins is a self-employed housecleaner originally from Brazil and living for thirteen years on Martha's Vineyard, an island off Massachusetts. I ask her, as I ask everyone, what she believes matters most in life. Her eyes well up with tears as she quietly says, "Peace . . . peace in your heart, peace with each other."

"Why are you crying?" I ask as my eyes also tear.

"Because we are looking at each other," and with two fingers, she points to her eyes and then to mine. "Too many people are lonely even when they are with others." We embrace for a long moment, and then she wishes for me the protection of angels on my journey. She has no idea how abundant in number those angels will be!

Something happens in the space between asking and listening. I believe it emanates from the vulnerability Regina points to, as when we truly see one another eye to eye. It frequently catches both participants off guard, the listener and the listened to. It hits me somewhere deep within my solar plexus. Such moments are fresh and new every time: microbursts of love, author Barbara Frederickson calls them, and they are often accompanied by tears of recognition of the other in ourselves.

I spent much of my early life trying not to be seen and therefore cultivated invisibility well into my adult years. When everything in my past was reinforced in my present, changing my perspective required Herculean effort. It is a long and gradual crawl towards the realization that I am enough. In the quiet spaces, I heard rumblings from my authentic self and began to make forward movement. Eventually, I realized I do not need to be carried or married in order to feel worthy. I slowly unclench the grip of self doubt and with a strong and steady gait, walk the way of Sarazan Greenwood.

I've learned so many lessons by giving audience to many wise people planted around this country. Sarazan is one of them. A crafter from Lubbuck, Texas, she offers, "If you want to feel joy in your life, you have to take the perspective of joy. No matter what horrible, torturous things can happen, we were given a higher mind to understand our conditions." She suggests that by understanding and choosing emotions from a higher place with courageous vulnerability, we can change everything.

So many living sages roam the planet. They are people we meet every day. That's you and me, by the way. We just need to do the work to rediscover what we already know, what has been passed down through the ages and spliced into our souls . . . to be true to our central selves. And you can't fudge it, either. Mat Wyble, the philosopher and darn good barista of Mat's Good Coffee in Panama City, Florida, explains, "People are like coffee. You can have a poor quality coffee, fill it with sugar and cream, and think you have something good." Really, it's just dressed up bad Joe.

Eric Lacey is good strong coffee.

He introduces me to the scenic wetlands of Alabama: one of the regions on my wish list. You just can't fully experience a place when you stick to the road. He, his wife, Theresa, and I cruise the Five Rivers Delta where the Mobile, Spanish, Tensaw, Apalachee, and Blakeley rivers flow into Mobile Bay.

Eric taxies his boat named T-Bag (okay, he's a strong cup of tea!) under the Cochran Bridge where in 1860, more than fifty years after slave trade was outlawed, a full ship of smuggled Africans sailed up the Mobile River. The ship owner hoped to evade federal authorities but was caught and brought to trial, though never convicted. Thirty-two of the people transported on his ship eventually settled in the region now called Africatown.

I love that he exposes me to that history. It is important to see. I am grateful for a backdoor tour of the Redneck Riviera—a local term, not mine. I am also touched by his painful admissions as he speaks about justice and other things he values.

As with the large majority of people I interview, family matters a great deal to Eric. Talking further, he waxes philosophical about the kind of world he'd like to see, and tears unsurprisingly appear. Simultaneously expressing guilt and frustration over harboring thoughts of vengeance, an emotion he would prefer to surrender to peace, he talks about war and issues of safety.

I think it's fair to say most people want a peaceful life. I suspect the people on that ship full of Africans only wanted a life free from strife—one in the place of their ancestral roots. How we create a peaceful existence is where we human beings may diverge in our thinking. Eric exposes the ongoing internal struggle between his strongly held beliefs of nonviolence and his very well studied assessment of what he concludes is required to rid ourselves of terrorism and injustice once and for all. On that evening, in so-called Redneck country, eating freshly shot and homecooked pheasant, Eric's internal battle lends itself to external tears.

"I feel relieved to talk about this stuff," he confides.

I believe each of us is exquisitely designed to use the challenges of our lives as catalysts. Whether presented with poverty, prejudices, physical or emotional ailments, or injustices—when our trials don't fit our coveted life view, we have the opportunity to learn and grow.

I am a late bloomer. I once wore a cloak of invisibility to anesthetize myself from the trauma and pain of my childhood. It wasn't until much later in life that I blissfully discovered a springboard held by each of my experiences. Rather than shying away from or railing against the roadblocks that confront me, I am curious to unpack the lessons that placed them there.

We are not dealt a transparent hand of cards when we enter life. Sometimes we aren't even aware of the game played or that there is a game. If we knew the cards we would draw or the cards in each other's hand, it wouldn't be interesting. We would have no motivation and would simply fold our cards and watch life play out in front of us while each of us remained invisible. We wouldn't experience the multitude of moves, bets, wins, and losses. But the more we engage, the more we learn and the more skilled we get—if we pay attention to the lessons along the way. The objective of such lessons is consistent. In my view, the teachings are almost always about love.

The stakes are high, but we can never win the jackpot if we aren't vulnerable to the many variations that life has in its deck. And it's nice to know we are not playing alone and there's always a crying chair at the table when the tears flow—and they undoubtedly will: some for sorrow but many for the joy of life's gifts under an overly tinseled tree of life.

*After a rowdy parade around town, the Bluebirds take a break at
Park Sans Souci in Lafayette, Louisiana.
They include, from left, back, Bonnie Grimsley, Lorita Briscoe,
Alice Boudreaux, a Channel 3 KATC cameraman,
walkers Marilyn Bush and Ginny Sassaman, and
Bluebirds Joe Fontenot, Jeanette Forestier, Patricia Delahoussaye,
Dianne LeBlanc and Dianna Toucheck with
Paula and Sharon Jolet from left, front, on
February 1, 2016 at 2,463 miles during
Leg 11 of the Happiness Walk.*

CLICKING MY RUBY SHOES

There is a joy in watching my own perspectives shift from what
I was conditioned to believe and giving myself the freedom to explore
new perspectives and find that there are even greater layers of happiness
I can give myself space to enjoy.

—Harry Uvegi
New York City

January 21, 2016
44.2601°N, 72.5754°W
Montpelier, Vermont

I'm sad. There are a few tender moments between me and Jeff,
even a prolonged hug which catches me off guard at the train
station. It is very out of character for him, especially since he hasn't
been communicative for years, not really connected with me. I'm
confused as to why he chooses that moment at long last to be
tender, to show his vulnerability. It's not until years later when my
eyes open to what it is actually all about. I believe it is his termi-
nus—his end of the line. It is also when I finally see that I don't
have to dwell anymore in the need to know. As Heather Jordan of
Jackson, Michigan, points out, "You're not a tree. Move!" In refer-
encing the secrets to life, even Albert Einstein said that nothing

happens until something moves. So I finally do as Heather and Einstein suggest. I set myself in motion. But at the moment, it's still 2016 and I have a train to catch.

I lug my backpack onto the passenger car and settle heavily into a backward facing seat watching my small town collapse into the cold winter morning. I'm on my way to Baton Rouge for leg number eight of an eventual seventeen. That doesn't mean I'm nearly halfway finished. I walk the legs in sections that have no predictable pattern except for their progress in a cardinal direction. Their timing depends on the seasons when geography warrants such consideration and family responsibilities and events, such as my father's doctors' appointments, birthdays, and graduations. The length of each trip is dependent on the same. Today I am headed for Louisiana.

January 29, 2016
30.5369°N, 91.7529°W
Krotz Springs, Louisiana

Louisiana's Arcadian region is the sweetest, hottest, and saltiest place on Earth bearing sugarcane, Tabasco's red peppers, and salt deposits. I enjoy each one of the sensory gifts the area has to offer as I make my way from Krotz Springs to Lafayette . . . and it all begins with Lisa Scrantz.

Ginny and Marilyn are walking with me when Lisa drives her red Hummer down the grassy bank towards the spillway. Her pink feather boa trails out her sunroof, and her horn blares. Our ride has arrived.

Lisa is spirited, loud, kind-hearted, and passionate about her family and her cows. She wears a perpetual smile on her face and addresses life head on. Laissez les bon temps rouler—let the good times roll—is Louisiana's creed, and Lisa fully embraces it. She is a perfect host for us.

Lisa sets us up in her paŕents' cabin on the Courtableaux
Bayou and treats us to boudin (rice and Cajun pork sausage),
thirty pounds of crawfish, jalapeno cheese balls, and King Cake.
When we are able to stand again, we rummage through her
trunks and costume ourselves in gold lamé outfits, feathered
masks, and beads. Then we mosey on down to New Orleans
for the Krewe of Cleopatra parade. It takes us two hours to get
there in what took me seven days to walk. My head spins with
the speed. Beads, coins, trinkets—we festively collect it all. Of
course, Ginny will have to transport everything home. I have
a full backpack, and Marilyn cannot manage to carry even her
own luggage.

The night before their departure from Lafayette back to the
comfort of their Vermont homes, Marilyn stepped on a waxed
bench in stocking feet to turn on a ceiling fan. Her feet slid to
the floor and so did the rest of Marilyn. She fractured her left
arm, and since the initial set did not hold, she required surgery
and a cast months later: another souvenir from the road. Nevertheless, I learn the acquired treasures were brought out again
for her and Ginny's neighborhood Mardi Gras celebration the
following year. The good times continued to roll!

As I experience Louisiana, it claims the five happiest cities in
the United States—Lafayette ranking number one. Just behind
Lafayette are Houma, Shreveport-Bossier City, Baton Rouge,
and Alexandria—it's no wonder I don't care to move on. The
people, the bayous, the celebrations, the music, and King Cake
for breakfast all combine to make for happy living—that's if you
don't go off the beaten path to places most tourists don't see.

A few months earlier, I am in New Orleans: too early to
enjoy Mardi Gras but not the jazz, beignets, or chicory coffee.
Ken Jones and Janel Johnson, friends from my hometown of

Montpelier, and Sue Ganzak Carnill, a new friend and host from Panama City Beach, Florida, travel to join me. It is one of the handful of days I have a support vehicle, which makes getting to and from my starting and ending points seamless. That and my company are the only upsides to the day's route.

The four of us walk on one of the many systems of levees along the Mississippi River. We take in the sites of one mega-industrial plant after another. The petrochemical corridor, that's how the stretch between New Orleans and Baton Rouge is known. To locals, it is straightforwardly called Cancer Alley.

Each of the buildings we pass is equivalent to the length of fifty-three football fields or, according to my loose calculations, a little over one hour long. I measure everything I do against my standard pace of three miles per hour.

The infamous area is known for its cluster of cancer patients with four of Louisiana's ten most serious chemical releases located here. Yet the pipes, ducts, and channels have their own bend towards beauty as they weave around an ancient cemetery like weeds of progress encroaching on an abandoned garden. Worthy of pictures, I think.

Three short and loud siren blasts cause me to jump. As I swivel around, two very stern-looking security guards step out of their patrol vehicle to ask, "Why are you taking pictures of this place?" Unique beauty or not, I accommodate their request (it really wasn't a request) and delete the photos on my phone camera as they look on. It was, after all, the very same day as the tragic bombings in Paris, and a high alert status was justified.

Another officer greets us less than a mile down the levee after we hear from what sounds like a bullhorn, "Pedestrians on the rubble. Pedestrians on the rubble." He hails from the nuclear power plant to our left, "Just checking in," he says politely. Eventually the local sheriff arrives in his patrol car. Sheriff Champagne quickly assesses our harmlessness and jokes about how we are causing a lot of trouble while he cautions us, once again, against photography before he sends us on our way.

They rigorously guard the chemicals that poison nearby waters. If only as much effort were put into protecting the health of people and the environment, I wouldn't have the following story to share.

January 31, 2016
30.2241°N, 92.0198°W
Lafayette, Louisiana

Two days from Lisa's fun farm, Ginny, Marilyn, and I reach the Happiest City in America. Jeannette Forestier hosts us for three nights. That's three nights of gumbo, étouffée, wine, and laughter. Jeanette is a member of the Bluebirds, a celebratory group that transforms humdrum into heavenly and mundane into merriment. They dance together, share stories together, parade around town, sing loudly, and are genuinely happy to be alive.

The Bluebirds are a group of cancer survivors.

We gather at the home of Cecile, Jeannette's best friend. There's more King Cake and more wine. We are here to celebrate the life of Cecile, who, I am told, lived her days to the fullest and made every moment count. She died the previous year, leaving a powerful legacy of friendship and positivity. "Live like Cecile" is one of the group's mottoes. Other sayings they live by include "It's all temporary" and "There's no U-Haul behind a hearse."

Indeed, it is and there isn't.

As the bow-tied waiter at the Camellia Grill in New Orleans where Lisa takes us says, "Life is precious. I get to wake up every morning and kiss my children on their heads." Some of us don't. The Bluebirds understand that fully, so they choose to live each day like Cecile.

Marilyn and Ginny go to bed while Jeannette and I stay up way too late talking—me in my near-Boston accent, she in her beautiful Cajun dialect which I could listen to all night and almost do. Except for the cancer, it is uncanny how our lives parallel one another. Before the night closes, she feels like a sister. A few nights later, we are the ones with whom she shares her birthday. There are feathered masks and theatrics at Randol's eatery where we indulge in crawfish bisque and cornbread, Zydeco music, and Cajun two-stepping in the round.

I suppose when faced with a life-threatening condition, time takes on a new dimension. There is no space for being anything but the vibrant person you are. Since the quantity of one's life is tangibly vague, the Bluebirds seem to counter the uncertainty by assuring the quality of every moment. The next day, we don more feathers and anything sparkly and parade around town singing happy songs to anybody who will listen or nobody at all. I am uplifted by the joy the group exudes and am in awe of their complete and utter joie de vivre.

I see it again in Omaha, Nebraska, when I meet Wendy at the Radial Café over breakfast and a good cup coffee. Wendy tells me the only way she overcame two bouts with cancer is through the fellowship of people within her circle. As a send-off to her two breasts the night before her mastectomy, Wendy proudly flashed her bosom to the entirety of her community, expressing thanks for the time she wore them. Celebrate what you have when you have them—move on after you've lost them, her actions say.

I pause my journey in the Pelican State (I didn't see many pelicans along Cancer Alley!) when it becomes clear my father is not going to survive his latest bout with small cell carcinoma of the lungs. He has already kicked cancer of the prostate, thyroid, and brain and lived four years longer than the oncologist's prognosis.

I get to know him in a whole new way during his last months. He tells stories from his childhood I had never before heard, and we play cribbage until the failure of his eyesight makes that simple pleasure impossible. He opens up emotionally and shares shocking details about my mother that put some meat on the bones of my childhood. He never complains. He takes each day as it is given—good and bad.

My dad is a singular Bluebird.

His doctors all point to his positive attitude as the medicine that prolongs his years on Earth. There is no doubt in my mind he takes total charge of his life and, it turns out, his death.

July 22, 2017
The Day Dad Died
Shrewsbury, Massachusetts

It is the last day of his life. Chris and her husband, Al; my brother Vern Johnson, sister-in-law Mary, and I are all gathered at my Dad's house while my older sister, Pamela Johnson, makes quick plans to fly up from her home in Mexico. We are all familiar with my father's wishes. More than anything he wants his four children under his roof one last time.

Pam's travels take a while. She has many details to manage and connections to make. Dad is already breathing through his mouth, a sign of imminent death I recognize from having midwived my mother's passing six years earlier.

It is late evening when Pam finally arrives. She and Dad have their private moment together. Though he never appears to regain consciousness, I sense he revels in her presence. We say our goodnights with long, knowing hugs and go to bed for what we anticipate will be an arduous tomorrow. My bed is the armchair where I've been sleeping next to Dad's rented hospital bed in his den due to his frequent medication regime.

After his second dose of the evening, believing it to be an auspicious number for transitions, I set the alarm to 5:55 in the morning.

The alarm never goes off. Pam shakes me awake at 6:10, and it is immediately clear my father just made his crossing.

All his children under one roof.

His death. His timing.

Relieved to end my snowy drive from Vermont with everything I salvaged from my marriage neatly stacked into sixty-square-feet, I swing my small frame down from the U-Haul truck onto icy asphalt. "You're a bad ass!" I hear.

No, that would be my Dad, but compliment taken.

I went directly from caring for my father back to the road a year later. In the meantime, I sold the house with nearly everything in it to Jeff. It's not until Valentine's Day, 2019—two years since I last stayed in my home—that I finally negotiate a date to claim my things. Truth is, I had no desire to move stuff to my father's and then again when I decide where I'm going to land, so the delay is an unforeseen advantage.

I leave a lot of baggage behind—there's no U-Haul behind a hearse. For years I've managed well with only what I could carry on my back, so I have little use for fluff. Most things don't matter anymore, though my sister Chris is amused by the things I do value as she helps wrap, stuff, and tape boxes:

- stockpiles of rocks, feathers, shells
- a pleather unitard once owned by Lana Turner and given me by my great aunt from Las Vegas
- a gold-beaded wedding headdress gifted by Uzbek visitors on tour in Vermont
- a sealed family time capsule put together by my children
- my handmade drum crafted by a local shaman, and

a ten-foot, front-yard peace pole that I personally carved with May Peace Prevail on Earth in four languages—French, Arabic, Yoruba, and of course, English—each sentimentally connected to my family

Among the material goods I leave behind are photo albums, the growth chart etched into the door frame to mark my children's passage through their youthful years, and the compost bin I received as an anniversary present. I couldn't retrieve the coveted crystals buried around my ceremonial fire pit under two feet of fresh snow, so I leave them to bless the house I love—the home and the life that are no longer mine.

July 2018
A Cross Country Trip On Wheels

My lifelong friend Cheryl is with me as we celebrate our sixtieth birthdays in 2018. We met in first grade, and she has been with me through every one of my life's ups and downs and twists and turns. That includes being one of the greatest cheerleaders of the Happiness Walk. She walks with me in Vermont, Massachusetts, and New York, often with a support wagon and taking excellent care of my wine and hosting needs. She is the kind of lifelong friend everyone deserves.

We are on a much-anticipated girls' road trip. Cell coverage is spotty, but the call from Daniel's Insurance Agency comes through. "Is the house empty?" an agent asks, referring to my father's mortgaged house left to me and my three siblings. It is the place I temporarily call my home, though it has no essence of me in it.

I explain that the house is my legal residence, that it is not at all empty but rather full of memories and materials now owned by me and my siblings. Of course, she knew that because we had previous dealings right in her office. We exchange pleasantries and hang up.

It's been nearly a year since Dad died, and we're still dealing with multiple financial and legal entanglements. I am grateful to my siblings for a place to live while I figure out my next steps. My life has been in transition for years. With one stake in Vermont, one in Massachusetts, and one on the road, I can't yet consider a permanent home. It scrambles my head to think in those terms, and my whole body resists.

Two days later, I get a text from my brother Vern that he received a notice from Daniel's Insurance in the mail. For no conceivable reason, the company cancelled our policy. And it had already been canceled when they called me! Consequently, the bank had no choice but to call in its loan, since the house was no longer insured. Vern, an astute business executive, explains how he attempted to correct the situation but to no avail. It forced all our hands to move sooner than we anticipated on our plan.

"I'm moving quickly to buy the house," wrote Vern.

That had been our long-term hope. "I need your agreement to sell your share of the estate in writing. Please send ASAP," read the text.

I'm three thousand miles away from the epicenter of that rip in my safety net, and it jolts me. The last shred of conventional security I owned is swept right out the door, leaving no firm place for me to stand. I look beyond my toes and see just one gaping void. The space beneath me is just that—space, and I'm falling into it. As I will do eight months later on a literal Pacific Coast cliff, I reach for any small outcrop to keep me from plummeting, only on the present occasion, there's no beach below to break my fall.

In one year's time, I've lost my marriage and, because of that, extended family, my home, my community, and several friends. The loss of my father was expected, but naturally sad and painful. I attempt to manage the cascade of losses with perspective and as springboards: *Celebrate what you have when you have it. Move on after you've lost it. Learn the lessons within the losses.* Nevertheless, I am blindsided by the most recent undoing. I'm sucker punched, and the wind has not returned to my defeated lungs.

I have no plan because I didn't know I needed one—not just at the moment, anyway.

Invisibility creeps over and around me once more.

I'm startled by my outrage. I thought I left that behind with my other baggage. Though I've been leading a nomadic lifestyle, I haven't exactly been homeless.

I need to adjust. I need to let my emotions catch up to my faith and my abilities.

I know I will be fine.

I am fine. Just give me a minute.

Breathe.

I'm scheduled to be "home" to attend a September wedding before I fly to Yakima, Washington, on my way to walk to Salt Lake City by Thanksgiving. The notion of being without a place to return to, to call my for-now home, disconcerts me. It doesn't take very long before I settle into it, though, and revise my outdated Excel sheet. I'm becoming skilled at bumps in the road, I notice.

Once a thin web of safety materializes beneath me, I am confronted by questions new to me, questions that many people who are truly homeless must face. Where will I receive my mail? What address goes on my driver's license, soon to expire?

Where do I register to vote? What address do I use on the many documents that require one? I never realized how often we must provide that information.

Notwithstanding, I am rich in relationships and resources. I can figure things out in time. I also realize that, as someone without a home, I'm asking privileged questions. I'm not asking where my next meal will come from.

I know I should consider myself lucky—and I do. But the sting takes a while to subside. And it stings anew every time someone asks, "Where do you live?"

Where do I live?

The road—my turf . . . that's where I live.

I find my home in every moment as do the Bluebirds, as did my father. What I call home is no longer dependent upon a permanent structure nor on cardinal coordinates but, rather, it travels with me. And, I like to think that when I leave this Earthly plane, a beautiful and light-filled home awaits me.

For now, this is how it is meant to be. Just me. Walking. A toothbrush and tent in my backpack. No house or car or stuff to weigh me down. No one to whom I am unduly tethered. No place I need to be.

Ahhh . . . this is what freedom feels like.

So, that's how I finally reply when asked where I live, "The road is my home."

And it feels perfect.

Life clearly has its own divine plan. It unfolds as a beautiful spring rose planted in one's garden: slowly, gently, beautifully. Had I not been separated from my husband, had I not given up my job to have the flexibility for the walk project, had I not discarded my material securities for the freedom to move around at will and then going where I was needed most, I would not have the memories of precious last months with my father. I would not have met wise philosophers in Lumberton, Fairhope, Lafayette, or Lubbock. Most strikingly, I would never have discovered what the Naked Cowboy uncovered—true freedom.

As my host Eli Frank of Lincoln, Nebraska, said, very little of happiness "is based in material possessions but rather more so in our experiences. I would say most people I've talked to at the end of their life would not look back and talk about things they've purchased but about experiences they had, the places they traveled, and the people they impacted."

I would guess people talked mostly about the ones whose eyes they had looked into.

Even more succinctly, Gigi of Brookfield, Vermont, says our attention "should be on experiences. It should be on the quality of life, not quantity of life."

Having learned so well from my father, I would add—the quality of one's death.

October 26, 2018
42.9549°N, 115.3009°W
Glenns Ferry, Idaho

It is here where I say my final farewell. I love this man so dearly and cannot fathom a future without him. I kneel on the banks of the beautiful Snake River, barely able to see through my tears, and scatter his ashes into the rushing water, just as he would wish—sending him home.

The ashes are not my father's.

Paula, left, and Nic Blouin, aka Biker Chic Nic,
head out en route to San Francisco from the Burlingame, California
home of their host Linda Stoik on
November 12, 2017 at 2,922 miles during
Leg 11 of the Happiness Walk.

OUTSKIRTS OF HOPE

I hold nature sacred. I feel that this planet is our church, and we're all members of its community.

-Wren Davis
Eugene, Oregon

Like a child, I grow into my newfound autonomy, at first navigating my companionless walk in baby steps. In short time, my days consist of quietly tenting behind bushes in the backyards of churches, eating breakfast pizza off gas station rotisseries, and urinating on the side of the road—rattlers be damned!

Ahhh . . . this is what freedom looks like.

As a novice student of simple living, I require more than confidence. I need a lot of instruction and coaching. I get that from my new friend, Biker Chic Nic.

I hardly know how I did it, but up until Santa Fe, New Mexico, thirty-five hundred miles into my nonlinear trek, I depended solely on hosts or motels for lodging, which included the entire width of Texas and towns with populations as low as eighteen people. Some points on the map were so small that I interviewed a quarter of the residents of one community. Caprock, New Mexico, held the distinction through to the finish line.

I had long since evolved into being comfortable as a solo walker, but despite the remoteness of roads so far, I know I will need an upgraded model of self-sufficiency as I approach even more desolate and arid stretches.

May 28, 2016
35.6870°N, 105.9378°W
Santa Fe, New Mexico

My needs are fulfilled when Nic Blouin tracks down our booth at the most lively and vibrant farmer's market I've ever experienced. She says she heard me on Mary Charlotte's "Radio Café" program on Santa Fe's public radio station and felt inspired to find me.

My Vermont friend Ginny had flown in for a couple of days as did then GNHUSA president, Beth Allgood, to promote the rollout of a new Charter for Happiness, another project for building momentum around GNHUSA's goals, and to procure signatories while at the market.

Biker Chic Nic is already on board with our vision. Well-tuned to the environment, she walks her talk about caring for our planet. Better put, she bikes her talk. Nic doesn't own a car and uses her bicycle as her primary means for getting around. Over the years, that entailed several transcontinental treks on her bicycle, which affords her a wealth of experience in low impact camping.

"Can I join you?" she asks.

That surprises me, because as far as I can tell, she has no interest in walking. But, she is glad to trade a pair of walking shoes for a pair of tires.

This is about to get more interesting!

Nic is not the only people-powered person whom I get to know. In 2014, I was honored to meet Dr. John Francis, the Planetwalker, who, in addition to relying on non-motorized transit for twenty-two years, spent seventeen of them in silence. He would later escort me into Boston in 2019 on my final day of the Happiness Walk and inspire my following tiny walk in silence to Vermont.

Dr. Francis is a giant in the worlds of pilgrimages and environmentalism. Plus, he is a gentle and kind spirit. I am curious to understand what drives people like Nic and John to make such unconventional choices. Although I have not learned their full stories, someday I hope to. Certainly, their examples fuel mine.

Nic and I discover we have a lot in common—we even share a birthday (the day, not year). Though I am several years her senior, Nic is definitely wiser when it comes to all things outdoors. Over a holiday break, she counsels me on purchases ranging from tent gear to rain jackets. She has done her homework about balancing the quality of items with cost and ounces with size. That's how I figure out how to make the transition into campgrounds, a practice that soon morphs into stealth tenting—the art of camping under people's noses and around city ordinances.

Nic joins me for 360 miles across Arizona. We are a pair. I walk. She cycles.

She travels ahead and, to direct my footsteps, leaves me organic arrows and happy faces made of sticks, stones, and road debris to make me laugh. I admire her spontaneity. I admire her ability to care for herself. But most especially, I admire her humor.

"I need to tell you," she confides, "I may just disappear someday." We do have a lot in common. Some days I want to disappear, too. I kinda do when I take off my vest. Nic, on the other hand, takes off on her bike.

Sometimes we don't see one another for days and then rendezvous at a predetermined destination to share our adventures. Nic experiences volume. I experience depth.

We both experience more than people in cars.

I am the only one who experiences the owl.

October 28, 2016
33.9698°N, 112.7302°W
Wickenburg, Arizona

There is no such thing as a side road here. I mostly travel along the highways and share my "sidewalk" with truckers. The speed limit calls for a reasonable 65 mph in Arizona, which means you can add 15 mph for sparse passing vehicles. That translates into the only breeze and relief from the full-on-heat of sun and pavement. Grateful the shoulders are mostly accommodating, I take care not to get pulled in by the suction each triple trailer truck generates.

It's late October, but summer hasn't loosened her grip as the temperature climbs to 104 degrees. I drink lots of water and am still feasting on a family-size pizza carried in my hip pack for the third day. It's getting quite ripe but provides me required calories, albeit greasy ones.

Perhaps the owl is also vulnerable to the oppressive heat. As I top a small rise on US 60, I am first surprised by hieroglyphs directly to my left on a large boulder. They stop me in my tracks, and I am mesmerized for several minutes.

Who made them?

What do they mean?

What did the author believe was worth such a permanent, painstaking inscription?

Will I ever have anything that worthy to carve in stone or permanently scribe on my body?

And . . . do motorists know what they're missing as they speed past at 80 mph?

As I stand in silent reflection awed by encounters I get to have on the road, my eyes catch a tiny movement just ahead and west of me. There, tucked into a small rock outcrop in the only shade for twenty miles, sits a one-eyed great horned owl silently staring me down. She never flinches as she sits so very still barely ten feet away, camouflaged within the boulders. Our three eyes lock. We stay connected like that. Untold moments tick by: me unable to look away, she tolerating me for an unknown reason.

Unlike the squirrelly roadrunner of yesterday who scampered away as soon as it knew me, and since we appear to be the only two living creatures on the same lonely stretch of pavement, my reverence for that raptor deepens. With her permanent wink, Owl declares herself my newest spirit animal. I will need her wisdom for what awaits me upon my return home. Forebodingly, the presence of Owl announces change.

Eventually, I push through dense heat and to find elusive shade. Sixty miles west of Wickenburg proper, I come across a sign that reads "WELCOME TO HOPE, AZ."

What a lovely name for a town, I think.

On the other side it reads "YOUR NOW BEYOND HOPE." Grammatical error or not (and there's disagreement about its intentionality), the sign makes me chuckle . . . until I realize there isn't a town which means there is no shade or drink or ice, at least not at that crossroad or anywhere within sight. I veer north onto AZ 72 towards Bouse, where my GPS tells me there is an RV park—just beyond Hope. One long day past Bouse lays California, my nineteenth state and a symbolic marker for me: the state where I was born, where my second daughter resides—and my cross-country goal, the Pacific Ocean.

Recreation vehicle trailer parks rarely allow tenting, but there are no camping options, and I don't want to spend money on a motel. Additionally, according to a local, the police refer to Bouse as "the worst town in the county of La Paz" and say that the motels attract sketchy activity. "Everyone here's a crook and a thief," says Randy, the WWII vet sitting outside a rundown motel.

I think I'll take my chances and speak to the sympathies of the RV park manager.

A golf cart pulls up behind me as I approach the office door. "I can't let you tent here. State rules. But if you're willing to do a little work, you can stay in one of the trailers over there," says Charlene as she points north towards a group of RVs.

Bingo!

"The owner died in it a few weeks ago. It has to be cleaned and emptied for sale. He left it in pretty rough shape."

Bust!

"I'll take it," I find myself saying.

Initially, I think it isn't as bad as Charlene made it out to be. I am wrong. The RV has been sitting vacant and all closed up in the heat wave. I set my bags down, scurry to the nearest store—the only store—and purchase cleaning supplies.

The occupant of the trailer was an elderly bachelor who didn't believe in routine cleaning, including his bathroom. Dishes were piled in the sink, everything disgustingly sticky and caked in rancid food scraps. I cleaned or discarded enough of the major offenses to make it tolerable-enough for the night. Exhausted from five hours of holding-my-breath, dirty work on top of a full day's walking, I drink a semi-cold beer, eat three packages of crackers from the not-very-well-stocked store, and collapse into my sleeping bag. I don't dare lie on the questionable RV mattress.

Sleep doesn't come easily, so I'm up with the beautiful sunrise and meet my neighbor Bill and his dog Happy over coffee under a tree.

"Have you ever heard of Peace Pilgrim?" he asks before he fetches the book he travels with, *Peace Pilgrim: Her Life and Work in Her Own Words* compiled by five friends, one of whom was one of my hosts. She died in 1981 after years of peripatetic teaching about peace as medicine for a sick world.

If you were to ask me to chronicle one defining moment of my entire trip around the country, I couldn't. There are simply too many. But if I were prodded until forced to recount just one, I would speak of three—three people to be exact: Richard Polese, Bruce Nichols, and John Francis, the Planetwalker. Richard is among the founding members of the Friends of Peace Pilgrim and is one of the compilers of the book Bill travels with. He hosted me in Santa Fe, where I slept on the same bed Peace Pilgrim slept on . . . an occasion I could never forget.

And then there's the serendipitous moment in Connecticut when I unexpectedly connected with Bruce Nichols, who delayed his travels to a Peace Pilgrim event in order to generously host me and another walker and old friend Cecelia Roberts. Both gentlemen—along with others—continue to share Peace Pilgrim's life work with the world. Until I've distributed them all, I carry much smaller, pocket-sized versions of her book given me by Bruce as inspiration and to share her words with those interested. In a nutshell, her message is, "This is the way of peace: overcome evil with good, falsehood with truth, and hatred with love."

Simple. To the point. Inspired. Just like the woman herself.

I don't know who gave me my first book, but if it's you, please remind me, and thank you! I read it years, perhaps decades, before I ever thought about walking. While there is so much to admire about Peace Pilgrim, the thing that struck me most and stays with me today is her authenticity, how she so clearly lived in accordance with her beliefs and values like so few I've ever known.

Not so simple.

As I do with Forrest Gump, I travel roads Peace Pilgrim traveled, meet people Peace met, and experience God's hand much as Peace did. She is my North Star. She's who I look to for guidance while I attempt to live as my authentic self or, to paraphrase her infinite wisdom, as I strive to attain inner peace and die, utterly die to myself.

I needed to meet Bill. I need a reminder to pay attention to my personal quest and not just the mission of GNHUSA. I don't know much of Bill's story, but I surmise he's come to just outside of Hope to die.

The tree we sit under actually glows in the photo I took of him. I love trees, and I notice them. I thank them, and yes, I hug them, and yes, I'm from Vermont. This tree, Bill tells me, is special. He believes it cured Happy's cataracts, and he hopes it also heals what's ailing him.

I pray it does.

Later, by car, Bill drops water jugs along my route to relieve me of the extra weight. I cover the twenty-one miles to Parker and return to the trailer on the back of Bullfrog's motorcycle for a second "free" night's lodging. I dry heave as I squeamishly tackle the bathroom, then return to the kitchen where I find Buddhist flags and incense as I empty out drawers. I assume the deceased owner, whose name I sadly do not know, had Buddhist leanings, so I string up the flags, burn some incense, light a candle, play mantras on my phone, and I pray for him, too.

As Peace said, "Do the things that need to be done. Do all the good you can each day. The future will unfold."

Hopefully you get through it without vomiting.

Nic and I part just before leaving Arizona. We've relaxed in Show Low with an old work friend, Vivian Cullen, nearly burned down a fire station in Kohls Ranch while cooking dinner on a Bunsen burner, served Navajo Tacos at Vernon's Community Center, and danced at an eighth grade school fundraiser in Aquilla. By some quirk of fate, we even found a roommate in Pie Town and a host in Phoenix with whom we all share birthdays.

Nic and I travel well together, we play well together, and we laugh together. We are in sync, or as Forrest Gump would say, we are just like peas and carrots.

We will walk/bike together one more time as I head up the coast of California where Nic will meet Sue, my new friend from Florida, and we will all fall in love with our host, Richard Murdock, aka Doc.

October 6, 2015
29.9480°N, 85.4180°W
Mexico Beach, Florida

Suzanne Ganzak Carnill loves tiny things. Colorful ceramic trinkets, miniature glass-blown animals, small memorabilia and baubles: they are the memories Sue gathers as she walks. Her enthusiasm for collectibles equals that of a spirited young child. Every knickknack embodies the sparkle she lost several years ago when her husband Greg was tragically hit and paralyzed by a jet ski.

I walk barefoot along the white quartz shores of Mexico Beach, Florida, the day before we meet. I catch a strong whiff of coconut sunscreen as tourists pass by. Blue umbrellas from local hotels dot the beach. There are coffee shops, restaurants, gift stores, and happy faces.

It is October, but the days are still sunny and beachworthy. It is also exactly three years to the day in 2018 until a Category 5 hurricane will decimate the vibrant coastal town. There will be no recognizable street corner nor landmark when I return to bear witness to the storm's wrath. The hotel room gifted me in

2015 lies at the bottom of the gulf. I do not know where the people are.

Sue and I watch Hurricane Michael play out on television in Union, Oregon, where she joins me for the fourth time since Florida. It is not the first nor will it be the last occasion that wind, water, or fire flex their muscles in my direction. Hurricane Sandy devastated Manhattan and Staten Island one month after I walked through. New Orleans was still reeling from the impact of Hurricane Katrina when I arrived on its tenth anniversary.

I walked in Marshalltown, Iowa, on the first anniversary of a destructive EF-3 tornado that blew through the downtown, and I witnessed Santa Rosa, California five months after debilitating fires decimated entire neighborhoods leaving only smoke and ashes behind. Hurricane Michael will slam Sue's hometown of Panama City Beach and surrounding coastal towns as will subsequent hurricanes over the years. Weather reports develop into forecasts of whether or not you lose everything you own or, heaven forbid, someone you love.

And then there's Nebraska. But I'll save that for later.

In 2015, Sue, a massage therapist by profession, introduces herself as a walker. On the first night she hosts me, I receive an unparalleled massage, the most relaxing and therapeutic I've received up to that very moment. She is not only skilled but also bright, personable, and in excellent physical shape at four years my senior.

Walking the country is her ultimate dream, so when her friend informs her I am in town, she flings her life open to my every need. We walk a little along the Florida Panhandle, and before I move on, we make plans to reunite down the road. Rather than traveling to Ireland for a long-planned, well-deserved vacation, Sue travels to New Mexico where we walk the dry rural road from Albuquerque to Pie Town—a far cry from the greens of the Donegal Mountains, the Pan Celtic Festival, and the Biddy Early Brew Pub.

A wide brim Boonie hat adorns her light blonde curls that kiss her shoulders. Jewelry splashes her ears, neck, and wrists. Her t-shirts honor sixties rock bands, and bright red lipstick highlights her smiling face. While her outlook is forever cheery, it becomes clear how well she has also dressed her disposition.

Blinded by water spray while operating a jet ski, a young woman hit Sue's husband as he waded in the shallow waters of Metropolitan Beach in Mount Clemens, Michigan. Greg suffered a traumatic brain injury that bound him to a wheelchair for several years before he died at the youthful age of fifty-five, seven years before I met Sue. It is unacceptable to reduce a person's life to one traumatic moment, and I apologize to him and Sue for brevity. I hope that someday Sue will share the incredible story she has within her, so I shall say just a little more.

Sue is adept at remaking herself. Leaning on her many talents and outgoing persona, she is a police officer—turned NBC affiliate sportscaster—turned Catholic Television Network producer. When her life turned upside down in 1995, Sue moved Greg from Detroit to the more hospitable climate of Florida, studied non-traditional nutrition, became a licensed massage therapist, and until his death cared for, advocated for, and lived for Greg.

Sue lives up to her introduction as a walker. She keeps up with my pace and never complains. My Excel sheet requires no modification to receive her company. Sticking to my schedule matters to me because what happens on one day of the walk has a rippling effect on future days, including the amount of time I get to spend with my family. Sue intuits it, and I am grateful.

Sue shows up prepared for anything. She travels with two suitcases, four bags, and three plastic bins—one of them often loaded up with gifts for me. Fortunately, she also brings a vehicle. "How can I help most?" is her mantra. She schedules her trips so as to support me in the most remote places rather than the most exciting ones. I know she wants nothing more than to tie on her sneakers, but Sue understands when a support vehicle will further the goals of the project more than making miles under her feet, and she accommodates that objective. Furthermore, she anticipates needs—and sometimes desires. On one occasion in the high mountains of Washington state, she made a surprising pizza delivery!

All of it makes up for the fact that she's an ardent Tigers fan.

November 2, 2017
36.3714°N, 121.9017°W
Big Sur, California

Why is she moving so slowly? I wonder.

We are approaching the iconic Bixby Creek Bridge in Big Sur, California. Nic Blouin has also joined me as we explore the beautiful, dynamic, rugged coast. Sandy beaches, dramatic cliffs, tenacious yellow and orange flowers clinging to rocky precipices, pods of pelicans, and colonies of melodious elephant seals make for a picturesque hike up scenic Pacific Coast Highway. I've been looking forward to this part of the trip for a long time. Here is an instance where the actual playing out of a lifelong dream eclipses its anticipation.

While Bike Chic Nic wheels ahead, walker Sue lags behind most of the day. Her attitude remains upbeat, but over time I sense she's struggling. Not wanting to be a burden, she won't admit it. She's pushing through something, I suspect, and even she is not sure what. Her energy is low, and her breathing is strained. I question whether she's gotten out of condition. I soon learn that's not the case.

Doc hosts all three of us for two nights, but his place is not easy to get to. A landslide at Mud Creek buried the Pacific

Coastal Highway on May 20, 2017—ironically, my twenty-eighth and final wedding anniversary—even the cliffs trembled and gave way to the heaviness. I trek alone as far north as allowable on Highway 1 before meeting up with Sue and Nic. Together, we make a treacherous drive with Sue at the wheel over restricted fire roads. We skirt the closed section of highway to arrive at the southernmost section of open road on the other side of the landslide.

Driving on Will Creek Road proves a perilous, white-knuckle experience. Sue feels confident driving over the narrow byway with soft shoulder cliffs on the right and rockslides of its own in the middle. Nic and I are not. That says more about our phobias than Sue's driving. I escape the rented vehicle when we arrive in Gorda where Doc makes his home and happily rely on my own two feet.

Doc is an uber host. He is captain of the Nacimiento Fire Station of Los Padres National Forest, the densely forested region we just traversed. He is extremely hospitable and the state-magnets on his refrigerator tell the tale of the many Warm Showers cyclist travelers who would agree with me.

Firefighting is a challenging job, as we can all attest. For Doc, it includes separation from his wife for days on end as she cares for her aging parents on the other side of the hellish road. To counter the stress of his job, Doc employs "a pondering chair." In that place of refuge, he commits to breathing meditation and contemplates his personal goals.

He speaks about his desire to lead a more serene life within the noble one he has chosen. Doc's laudable capacity to give and care for others in his work, within his family, and in his spare time embodies a life of service that Peace Pilgrim would praise.

We stay in touch and postcards and magnets are mailed his way. When I finish my ten thousand miles, he sends me a photo of himself holding a banner "Congratulations Paula—you rock." Doc is a megalith in his own right.

In 2020, three years after Doc, Nic, Sue, and I meet, I receive a request from GoFundMe, an online fundraising platform I am familiar with and have used for offsetting personal expenses of the Happiness Walk. I read,

> Fifteen dedicated firefighters on Dolan Fire received injuries including burns and smoke inhalation while defending the Nacimiento Fire Station. The station was destroyed. Three were sent to the hospital and one is still hospitalized.

Doc was one of them. After recovering from a heart attack sustained during a solo pleasure hike just a year before, Doc was sent to a burn center to recover from injuries sustained through his work.

"I'm doing ok," he writes. "Hopefully, I can go back to work soon. Enjoy every day and live your dreams." He's arm-in-arm with several staff wearing blue scrubs and masked faces and smiles his engaging smile at the camera in the photo attached to his message. I have no doubt he had the staff all smiling beneath their masks, too.

I know Doc has the will to recover fully. I need him to. He has to be ready to join me when I return to cover the sixteen miles of the closed, mud-laden road I had to forgo.

When Sue stops eating and she can't get out of bed one morning, I am alarmed. By day's end, so is she. I manage to get her on a plane home, as she refuses to see a local doctor. I later learn of her fear that a hospital wouldn't release her to travel, and thus she would be stuck twenty-five hundred miles from her friends and family. She's probably correct. Still, it frightens me to put her on the plane in her compromised condition.

Sue arrives back in Florida where a friend immediately whisks her to a hospital directly from the airport. She stays in intensive care for an unconceivable six days and hospitalized for a total of nine. The doctors are stumped. They blindly attempt several interventions. Her vital signs continue to wave red flags, but no one fingers a cause.

"It doesn't look good," she relays weakly from her hospital bed.

I'm distraught. I don't know how to help.

I'm feeling guilty and culpable.

She wouldn't have gotten sick if not for me.

It takes months for Sue to get back on her feet. Luckily, she recovers through will and hard work—the same doggedness she embodied while she cared for her husband. Though a diagnosis is never identified, I fear the walk is inevitably enmeshed in the illness.

It takes months for me to regain my solid footing.

We've become good friends since Florida. We share a lot between the miles, and I confide in her as much as she confides in me, which is not like me. I am not comfortable talking about myself—which, by the way, makes writing a book quite an anomaly. I am far more comfortable being the interviewer than the interviewee, being behind the camera rather than the object of one.

In the long stretches of coastal California's pinion trees and pavement, I learn about the challenges and joys of caring for a loved one confined to a wheelchair, as Sue did with her husband, Greg. Sue learns about the struggles and gifts of my having cared for a parent with Alzheimer's. We both use our heartache as compost for growing into ourselves. I learn from Sue's faith. Sue learns from my grit. I revel in Sue's accomplishments and Sue in mine. That is what friends do.

I confide in Sue how difficult it is when the door is closed to talking with my daughters about their father and me. The subject of the divorce appears to be taboo. My daughters each has her own process, each of them different. If they need to talk with someone, it is clearly not me. I trust they have confidants in their life as I do with Sue.

It will take years before any semblance of normalcy returns—at least on my end. I am fragile when it comes to my daughters. I have no clue what they believe to be true or how to support them. It makes my heart ache. But I see they must pursue truth on their own terms, not mine.

I hope they see my broken pieces have mended. I hope they see a strong woman not bound by age, expectations, fears, or scarcity who dares to step into her calling—a mother who defies convention to forge her own destiny, a daughter who is present when presence matters most, a person with strong conviction, perseverance, and spirit—otherwise known as tenacity. I hope they see how much a person can choose an affirming path through adversity.

I can hope. And I share my hopes with Sue.

Like mine, Sue's brokenness also takes mending. She grows gracefully into herself as a woman who has lost her true love, and eventually she heals from the rogue illness never properly diagnosed that nearly took her life. Recovering from our respective brokennesses each takes faith, and both take years.

Sue joins me in Washington state just ten months after Big Sur, and her walking is once again dampened diagonally across the continent as she watches Hurricane Michael rip through her Florida town. A year later and back in top form, Sue joins me again whilst we walk her old stomping grounds in Detroit Tigers country. All in all, my friend joins me five times after Florida, and the novelty of our shared experiences never wears off. In between, we chat about our lives and exchange tiny tchotchkes, baubles, and bagatelles.

When Greg was liberated from the confines of his trapped body into an immortal world, Sue chose to publicly remember him with a Navajo prayer entitled "Night Way"and printed on his favorite blue t-shirt. The prayer is one that speaks to me deeply. It reads in part:

> With beauty may I walk.
> With beauty before me may I walk.
> With beauty behind me may I walk.
> With beauty above me may I walk.
> With beauty all around me may I walk.

I return home from out west, take down the Buddhist flags that hang around my Vermont house, say goodbye to my trees with big hugs, and invoke Owl and Peace Pilgrim: "Look inside for your truth. Your divine nature—your inner light—knows all the answers."

Until I fully embrace that wisdom, I use props.

"I was a real son of a bitch before I had a heart attack and bypass last year," says Steve at the Tallahassee Flea Market as he wraps camo paracord around the handle of a varnished hickory stick. "Now I'm trying to be a nice guy by feeding the poor. Hey, give me fifteen minutes and come back, won't you?"

I go about interviewing vendors and patrons alike before I return to finish my conversation with Steve. He hands me the beautiful walking stick with its gentle twists, strong curves, and spiral grooves cut by lost vines. "I want you to have this. As a gift. I'm trying to be kind."

That was September 27, 2015. Though I never thought to use a walking stick and while carrying one adds an awkwardness that often borders on frustration, at the times when it is useful, it is priceless. And it shows its practicality in several ways, frequently to enlarge my appearance when confronted by menacing dogs, and once when it suffices for a tightrope on the high cliffs of Redwood State Park.

You would think the walking stick would be an extension of myself after four years of exploring the country together. To leave it behind would be akin to forgetting to gather my arms before I get back on the road. But I do leave it behind several times during the walk. And even though I absolutely despise retracing my steps, we always find our way back to one another. It gives me confidence when mine is lacking and it gives me strength when mine is depleted. It is my sidekick for life—till death do us part.

With beauty may I walk.

I know I am blessed to have physical legs, blessed to make my pilgrimage, and stunningly blessed to shoulder the tribulations placed before me. Mine are minor challenges compared to those of others. I have seen the will and faith of individuals slay the incursions of adversity and stand firmly in their truth. I have high regard for those people—the ones like Peace Pilgrim, the Planetwalker, Sue, and the others who walk the planet with beauty. Each is a titan in my eyes. Some choose their path. Others, I learn in Louisiana, have it dropped in their proverbial or literal lap.

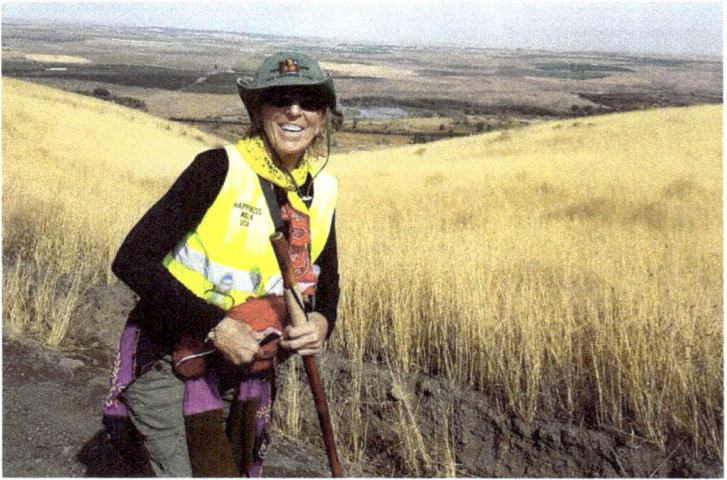

Sue Ganzak Carnill takes a shortcut through hills near
Wallula, Washington as she heads for
good food and a soft bed in Pendleton, Oregon on
October 15, 2018, at 6,366 miles during
Leg 15 of the Happiness Walk.

FLAP YOUR WINGS

*One thing I'm particularly thinking about after the discussion is
just how much happiness has to do with intent and action.
That it's not so much a place that you get and you sit there, but it's about
interacting—noticing things, being in gratitude, paying attention—
putting love into action in some kind of way.*

—Kathy Cummings
Highland Park, New Jersey

"Nothing will ever change. I keep myself busy so I don't have to think about things," says a customer at Kings Truck Stop and Casino in Barre, Louisiana. The man's life may very well play out according to his scripted view. I suggest that happiness could visit upon him if he weren't so distracted by counting his woes and instead counted his blessings—as does Mr. Steven who sees his glass as half full rather than half empty.

*January 30, 2016
30.5369°N, 91.7529°W
Krotz Springs, Louisiana*

I meet Mr. Steven eighteen miles from Kings Truck Stop. Both men, whom I earmark as around the same general age, live in the same general community—presumably with similar local conditions. Yet, Mr. Steven is an improbable optimist. We meet at his modest house on a beautiful bayou near the Atchafalaya River, he in his wheelchair on his accessible deck. Several years before, he was driving his wife, children, and another family member when a deadly accident ensued leaving the decapitated head of his wife—his love—in his lap. Others sustained injuries, including those similar to the ones that restrict Mr. Steven to his wheelchair.

He speaks frankly and gently.

As someone with paralysis from his chest down, he spends many hours in and out of hospitals and rehabilitation centers. "There are two kinds of people in the hospital, the ones who just give up and the overachievers. The difference between these two groups," Mr. Steven submits, "is having something worth living for." For him, it is the belief his wife would expect him to care for their children, which is exactly what he does.

Mr. Steven's resolve molded his purposeful progress. But for those who are alone or lonely or for those without a sense of purpose or meaning, physical and emotional healing from trauma may appear insurmountable. I later meet someone who devotes his professional life to changing those odds.

October 12, 2019
42.3806°N, 76.8733°W
Watkins Glen, New York

I introduce myself to Dr. Frank Bourke after a mid-October night of camping at Watkins Glen State Park in upstate New York. I managed to get through the evening by bundling in layers of clothing and putting handwarmers in each of my gloves and socks. At daybreak, finding Seneca Lodge just a couple thousand feet from where I pull up camp is a coup. That the place serves a hot meal and coffee next to a roaring fireplace is a stroke of luck.

Dr. Bourke breakfasts there with a group of friends and, since I am my mother's daughter, I overhear his conversation. As he stands to leave, I invite him to my table for a cup of coffee. I must look unusual enough, with my life on my back and all, that he agrees. I learn Dr. Bourke is the executive director of the Research and Recognition Project which he founded to investigate effective treatments for post traumatic stress disorder, PTSD. He tells me he and his colleagues have designed a five-hour protocol that cures, not tempers nor delays, PTSD. He tells me it happens without the use of pharmaceuticals and has a very high success rate with patients. He cites something in the ninetieth percentile.

I find that astonishing news, of course. If what he claims is only half true, there ought to be a public outcry to make his work mainstream. He cites "big pharma" as a barrier to changing national policies and practices that could bring relief to those wandering souls I meet in Everywhere, USA.

A distinguished looking man with a clean white beard and mustache under a black woolen western fedora and kind but sad eyes says, "My heart," (he begins most of his solemn responses to my enthusiastic, and perhaps naive, inquiries this way) "I'm getting ready to give in. I've been doing this for a long time. Corporate greed and our human condition are at play here."

As I finally get on the road at ten o'clock with his words resounding in my head, my feet are heavy. My legs are slow and shoulders slumped under the weight of my reflections. I have a long hilly day ahead of me to Ithaca. No matter. I stop a mile down the road and wait in a long line on the chance that Toby's Doughnuts is the place where I can nibble away my frayed edges (and perhaps find a winner to outrank Johnny Doughnuts).

Optimism, my heart tells me, can be buried under mudslides or drowned by the surging waters of hurricanes if one is not careful. Optimism can also grow, so says my new friend and host, Mark Weinsoff, in Goleta, California. As the 2020-2021 international president of Optimist International, Mark has an encyclopedia of knowledge about optimism.

"We know this world is not a perfect place. What makes us optimists is we believe we have the power to change the world for the better," Mark says. "What you do to make the world a better place and the relationships you build are what matters."

Club members nurture their optimism through meaningful and purposeful activity with a focus on youth. They are also of the mindset that bad things may happen, but isolated incidents don't need to bleed into other parts of your life.

Over the years, I've learned how to bandage my hemorrhaging negativity. I know that the heaviness of a dismal moment will eventually lift. I exercise my optimism muscles and practice the skills I need to return quickly to my set point because I've seen the damage internal trauma can otherwise pen in one's diary. I make the purposeful choice to nurture a positive attitude. That was not always true in my life, but I continue to have teachers.

I think about Ms. June zipping around in her big Monte Carlo from one volunteer job to the next in her Florida hometown. She seizes every opportunity to lift people up and to help in any way she can, even someone walking around the country in need of a place to rest her head.

For all her outwardly charm and apparent strength, Ms. June imparts a disturbing story of suffering. The list is long and painful. She has had five heart attacks and skin cancer and grapples with severe depression. She has two broken kneecaps, estranged children and grandchildren, and over the span of years was serial raped by her first husband who once lit her bed on fire while blocking any possible means of egress.

I used to think life was all peace, love, and light.

Ms. June has the biggest heart of anyone you will ever meet. She knows, possibly without understanding, that caring for one another, expressions of gratitude and generosity, and even the small act of smiling are the lifeblood of happiness. In her book *The Age of Miracles,* Marianne Williamson says, "When a butterfly flaps its wings near the tip of South America, it affects the wind patterns near the North Pole." In other words, Ms. June's localized acts of compassion dispatch a flurry of goodness across the planet.

Even Benjamin Franklin said, "The US Constitution doesn't guarantee happiness, only the pursuit of it. You have to catch up with it yourself." Ms. June does not let herself be defined by her past experiences, others' opinions of who she was or who she is, nor by what she's been told she is capable of. Rather, she catches her own happiness and, by doing that, she catches enough for us.

Like the wings of a butterfly, Ms. June breezed into my life to impart a generous gift in the haunted town of Monticello, Florida, and my life is much richer for having met her. "So, flap your wings," Ms. June might say. "Do it brilliantly, colorfully, and with purpose. Let your freak flag fly!"

I find some people just aren't comfortable with the level of optimism I've grown into. That has played out in the form of interventions in a few places around the country. They are well intentioned, for sure, and based in genuine concern and care. Typically, they go as follows.

"Hey! Hi! What are you all doing here?" or in the South "What y'all doin' down here?" I ask as I come in from a day's excursion and the room goes silent with my presence.

"Paula, we're here because we're all worried about you."

"About me? Why?"

"Because you don't seem to have a plan. You're leaving here tomorrow, and you don't know where you're staying. We're worried for you."

"Ohhhh," I exhale as it hits me. "I really appreciate your concern, and I certainly don't want to cause you any worry. I know what I'm doing is unconventional, but I'm safe—really! And I'm protected. Things always work out. I've been doing this for a long time."

"But, Paula. It's dangerous out there. Have you seen the news lately? You don't know this place. And you're going through some rough neighborhoods." And then the inevitable question, "Are you carrying?" I quickly learn that inquiry translates to, "Are you packing a gun?"

It's always the next town over.

I understand their view. Goodness knows, I've had my share of let-go-and-let-God moments when my daughters traveled to places around the globe not known for their high safety ratings, particularly for English-speaking beautiful and often unaccompanied young women.

"Mom, the insurgency is across the border."

It's always the next country over, I convince myself.

But I remain optimistic. I don't attempt to sway anyone from their perspective because it's difficult for others to shift their view if they aren't accustomed to trying on other people's shoes. I am touched by their warmth and do my best to alleviate stress levels, since stress is the opposite of what I've set out to achieve on the Happiness Walk. I express my gratitude for their safe harbor, then move on to my next destination. Wherever that may take me, I am safe, and I am protected.

Five years and approximately forty-five hundred miles into walking, I take to asking people if they have hope for a positive future, one that focuses on what matters most in life for them.

The replies tilt towards the affirmative mixed with a spattering of pessimism. I also hear a bit of ambiguity, with some saying they "hope to be hopeful," thus suggesting a lack of trust in their own aspirations. But the more common answer is "absolutely" or "you have to be hopeful," inferring its absence is simply not an option.

I do have hope, and more of it than when I first started the project. We may have a plethora of troubles laid at our feet and an ominous history to overcome, but I have borne witness to enough intelligent, thoughtful, and forward-thinking people and seen enough encouraging projects to sweep me off my feet and my worries with them. Whether it be Harry Uvegi's advances in biomimicry, Kathryn A. Flynn's New Deal proposal, Dr. Bourke's PTSD protocols, or Kurt Pipa's black soldier flies, the ingenuity that surrounds us is awe-inspiring. I find it especially true as seen in younger generations, and I believe my optimistic friend Mark would concur.

I call them systems busters because those Creatives don't rely on the same dimensional thinking I was raised on. Theirs is much more elevated and aspirational. They are not easily shaken by rules or failure nor by the complexity and cooperation today's solutions require.

I often find myself wondering how it is, with all our technological advances, we cannot provide the essential needs of food and clean water to all people in all places. Richard Witherspoon of Idaho Springs, Colorado, believes we can. Richard works on an entirely different plain than most. In search of the answers to origins of life, he engineers craft that perform exploration in deep space.

If we can design and land equipment on an asteroid traveling forty thousand miles per hour through outer space, surely we can satisfy the basic needs of people on our planet.

"Goodness doesn't particularly matter, because we are insignificant in the grand scheme of the universe, but in the short period of time we are alive, I think it is important to be good," says Richard. He believes *We the People* have the wherewithal to care for one another, but those who control our systems lack the resolve to shift resources towards that end, to do good.

I met a dentist in Santa Fe who told me he doesn't follow the Hippocratic Oath of physicians, "first do no harm." He tells me the ethical pledge he lives by is "first, do good." I think you might agree his would be a great foundation for designing our systems.

"We now have the resources," said Dr. Martin Luther King Jr. "We now have the skills, we now have the techniques to get rid of poverty. And the question is whether our nation has the will."

Surely our resources, skills, and technological know-how have increased in the past sixty years. It is an abomination we are still impoverished in our resolve.

Until such time as we insist each person be treated as our brother and sister, we cannot expect the tides to turn on their own. As Joan of Portland suggests, "We need to dialog to find common ground." I believe I've unearthed much commonality during the walk, but the conversations must continue to flow as regularly as the incoming tide.

Cultural change need not wait. The vitality of our communities isn't totally dependent upon high-level thinking or lofty intervention. It simply requires a change of heart. As one fellow wanderer, Chris Gale, puts it, "What kills people in the wilderness is the same thing that kills people in the jungle and in the urban environments: hopelessness." For that, there are wisdom solutions, and everyone can contribute. We need to transcend hope and touch faith as the sign so optimistically suggests, YOUR NOW BEYOND HOPE.

While visiting Santa Fe, the City of Holy Faith, I sit on a darkly varnished spruce pew in the Loretto Chapel as I stare at a spiral staircase remarkably suspended in air. By all accounts, it shouldn't exist. In the 1870s, the Sisters of the Chapel made a novena to St. Joseph, patron saint of carpenters. They prayed for a workable solution for safe access to the choir loft for the girls who sang there.

Their invocation was answered by a stranger who quickly crafted the stairway before he disappeared as inexplicably as he arrived. His thirty-three-step masterpiece is known to locals and pilgrims alike as the Miraculous Staircase, a stunning design that mystifies experts to this day.

The sisters had hope—or better put, faith, that their petitions would be answered. I have come to believe that prayers, intentions, visioning—however you choose to think of them—work, and the sisters knew that as their truth.

I wholeheartedly believe in prayer. I pray every day and often in my own homespun way. But it also takes doing to actually get things done. Faith is essential. Then one must allow faith to forge action—even if that action is to welcome the miracle that walks through your door. Faith alone is not enough. You must also be the carpenter of your circumstance.

My new artist friend in Santa Fe chooses to design her own fate in colorful ways. And, as it turns out, mine too! She sees me as I am—a wanderer with one toe in the ground.

Paula's Santa Fe, New Mexico, host and artist friend Cynthia Stibolt
displays one of her handcrafted angel cards on
September 18, 2016, at 3,510 miles during
Leg 10 of the Happiness Walk.

DANCING MARY

*There are days when I am more in my head
than I am in my shoes.*

—Gus Lacey
Fairhope, Alabama

June 1, 2016
35.6870°N, 105.9378°W
Santa Fe, New Mexico

I am getting ready to take the Rail Runner Express to the Albuquerque airport for my flight home when a radiant, tall woman with a full halo of beautiful white hair approaches me.

"Oh, my dear, we were meant to meet," says Cynthia Stibolt just minutes after introducing herself in the Santa Fe depot. She pauses dramatically and with great emotion continues, "In fact, meeting you is the cornerstone of this life!" meaning both hers and mine. I do not know what her proclamation means, but I'm curious to find out, so I accept an invitation to stay with her upon my return.

A few months later, we meet again on September 18, 2016, a 9-9-9 date. Though numerology intrigues me, the depth of my understanding is shallow. In short, it is obvious September is the ninth month of the year. The other nines equal the sums of the day (1+8=9) and the year (2+0+1+6=9). A quick internet search reveals that triple nines portend a death of the old self to fully express the person you are born to be, a rebirth. The phenomenon will show itself through service to others for the creation of a better world. Furthermore, the universe is here to guide you in the right direction.

The meaning Cynthia attributes to triple nines is "sleeping with the angels."

Hello, Universe. Hello, Angels. Hello, Cynthia!

Cynthia and I hit it off right away. "There's a reason, a season, or a lifetime that people are in your life," she tells me. Her voice is soft and calming as she conveys the things she is guided to disclose. As she speaks, I notice the ache in my neck that's been plaguing me for days has vanished.

Whatever the literal or figurative pain-in-my-neck was, it's history!

Looking ahead to my sixtieth birthday, I have a vision of dancing through my final decades of this life. My mother, Joyce, inspired my love of dance, and as an adult, I haven't done nearly enough of it. I remind you for a reason that will soon reveal itself. I will also share the following. Over the years, I have felt an almost tangible presence of an ethereal female guide. I feel protected and comforted by the being whom I have dubbed Mary. The name just feels right. She shares characteristics with my mother, but she is more than my mother or a mother. She is gentle, wise, and intensely loving.

Whether you believe in such things or not, it is fair to say that many of us have a pull towards all things fantastic. Fantasy films are highly popular with people of all ages, haunted tour businesses abide in every large city, and who hasn't grown up reading fairy tales? We seem to revel in the mystical and mysterious.

I have no interest in convincing you of my experiences except to ask that you suspend judgment and consider the possibility that we don't know everything there is to know and that not everything worth knowing is knowable. It's not a big stretch. We routinely observe holidays that celebrate historic miracles. We pray to invisible deities in all the world's languages with an expectation that we're heard. We throw salt over our shoulders to ward off evil, hear stories of spontaneous healings in violation of natural law, and can clearly view India's Kailasa Temple intricately and inexplicably carved out of a single rock from the top down.

An inordinate number of unknowns face us in this lifetime. They range from paranormal events to the wonders of quantum entanglement. Never mind what may happen tomorrow. Yet, we are often keen to dismiss what is right under our noses—or over our shoulders, should that be the case. To cast off such circumstances as mere anomalies is, perhaps, to be distracted from life's true nature.

While the simple act of taking twenty-thousand breaths each day is a miracle unto itself, I've also breathed in a spectacular statue that spontaneously emanated from a cave wall and an enlightened guru's hand imprint melted into rock, both in Nepal. They convince me to keep an open mind. Furthermore, when a wise soul recently coached me into a state of resonance that allowed me to bend an ostensibly unbendable metal object, my understanding of what is possible changed forever.

So when Cynthia, with all her intensity, proclaims our meeting holds some significance, I do not discount that as implausible. Upon my autumn return to her home in the Santa Fe hills, she advises me to immediately ditch my bags as she escorts me to her art studio. The stone walkway curves past flowerbeds and hedges—there are no hard angles to the sacred geometry defining the space. The inner sanctum is reverently staged with candles and meditative music, a soft contrast to the airport, train, and taxi I just abandoned.

Left alone to experience her art, I am instantly bathed in tranquility. Along the walls, methodically along the floor, and on tables are brilliant paintings of what Cynthia describes as "angels appearing in new and contemporary ways, as light-filled, unique beings, ever present and waiting for us to recognize them as true helpers and intermediaries."

They are stunning. I am captivated by their magnificence. As I shadow the sun's rays illuminating one radiant angel after another, the watcher in me moves through time and space. Just as the sun is about to nod beneath the horizon, it beams its last whispers of light onto the third eye of a colorful celestial being before it drops to her golden heart where it pulsates and fades.

The name of the painting is *Rebirth.*

Although angels have been captured by artists since the dawn of time, Cynthia's angels appear divinely inspired, captured by the artist with all their jewel-like robes, golden coronas, and glorious essences. Her brush is shepherded from one stroke to the edge of the ethereal sky with no evident awareness of the perfection intuited until her vision is exhausted and gratified. An angel conceived upon a virgin canvas.

Four years later, I have somewhat settled into stillness with a place to store my things and myself thanks to the extraordinary generosity of my sister Chris. Until such a time, owning a Cynthia Stibolt original made no logistical sense but as soon as it felt right, I contacted my friend to discuss the purchase of one of her pieces. We went back and forth to discern the most favorable one for me. She favored a painting of a golden *Earth Angel* with walking stick in hand. Of course, it seemed a natural for me, but I was more readily drawn toward one that reminded me of my visit—the apparition whose heart exploded with the last rays of the sun. As *Rebirth* had previously been sold, I opted for a similar one, a painting aptly named *Opening the Heart*.

A few weeks later, I tackle many layers of cardboard and foam with great anticipation only to unveil neither of the paintings discussed but rather one titled *Dancing Mary.* I'm perplexed and disappointed. I put the painting aside and choose not to contact Cynthia just yet. The following day I hang the inspirational art on my wall, its color likely to clash with the palette of the painting, but somehow it does not. I wait another two days before I phone Cynthia. By then it is clear: the painting was meant for me.

I have since crossed the sixty threshold in age, and I am still waiting to waltz. But Mary doesn't let me off the hook. My ever present guide and angel never fails to encourage me. Dancing in a frame on my sister's wall with colors contrasting, she reminds me daily to dance through the many hues of discord and to curate the radiance of my own masterpiece.

I need such reminders because I live my life way too soberly. I always have. When I took the VIA Character Strengths online survey several years ago, humor came in dead last out of twenty-four possible values on my test results. Ha—but, really not so funny!

Even the tag line for the Happiness Walk is *serious about happiness,* thus putting irony about the walk and the walker front and center for all to behold. Whenever my sister Chris gifted me pepper spray or anything that would provide her and my family a sense of promise for my well-being, she added a note that read "serious about safety." My demeanor is well established—even though I dress it in smiles.

Dancing Mary is the first thing I see in the morning (right before my first cup of coffee) and the last thing I see at night. She is a resplendent reminder to dump the seriousness and lighten up—lighten up to joy.

So, I once again change into a new pair of sneakers, lace them up tight, and gratefully acknowledge the absence of pebbles. I take notice of the place in my heart where a hole once dwelled but has become whole. A lifetime of synchronicities culminates into a growing understanding of my warrior self. Among them are the seen and unseen forces around me.

As Theodore Roosevelt said, "Be practical as well as generous in your ideals. Keep your eyes on the stars, but remember to keep your feet on the ground." Grand advice, though the stars are oh, so sparkly!

I take Teddy's advice seriously, of course, and call to my angels, "Please tell me what I need to know."

I pause to add grounded practicality. "And be specific about tomorrow's housing, please!"

Shanna Parker-Boutwell and Ms. June wait for Paula in front of the haunted Daffodale House in Monticello, Florida, on September 22, 2015, at 1,779 miles during Leg 7 of the Happiness Walk.

PURE FREAKIN' MAGIC

*Man's search for meaning has gone on as long as the world is old, and
I think that's one of the most fundamental components of what matters.*

-Melissa Morgan
Berrien Springs, Michigan

I love coffee! Ever since my early teens, I've had a romance
with coffee thanks to family gatherings around our kitchen table
on Sunday mornings. Aunt Carol drank hers black and steamy
hot with an ice cube. I wanted what she had except for the
superfluous ice cube.

I swoon at the aroma of coffee. Like one of Pavlov's dogs, if
I see a cup, I want a cup. More than mile markers measure my
distance, cups of coffee mark the progression of my day from the
coveted first sip in early morning to the last caffeinated kiss in
the evening. Coffee is my clock, my sustenance, my oxygen.

So much of my venture is geared toward finding my next rich,
bold, black, cup of java: preferably freshly ground French roast
beans steeped in a French press. I considered purchasing a travel-
sized press for my pack, but without the ability to heat water, it
would be a pointless addition to my gear.

As an alternative, I've taken to carrying my own mildly
satisfying instant coffee that I covertly add to sub par gas-station

blends or discreetly pour into a mug offered by an unsuspecting host. It boosts both the flavor and my spirits. Even though I calculate every ounce in my backpack, my instant coffee packets and steel carabiner coffee cup are my constant companions along with my hickory walking stick. Though I've never been a smoker, I've heard smokers get anxious when running out of cigarettes with no prospect of restocking. Substitute butts for joe, and you've named my undoing.

Coffee greases my joints, but water is my gasoline. In addition to my rucksack, I wear a hip pack on my front with a water bottle holder on either side. Of all I carry, water is by far heaviest yet most important to my survival.

April 24, 2016
32.2504°N, 101.4787°W
Big Spring, Texas

I'm walking outside Big Spring, Texas, in ninety-degree heat through farm country—not to be confused with Big Springs, Nebraska, where I will walk in scorching heat through farm country three years later.

Here I see my first tumbleweed. I wear a bandanna over my face as a shield from the churning dirt stinging my exposed arms and legs as dirt devils crisscross lanes before and behind me.

Though I started the day with two bottles of Gatorade and an extra bottle of water beyond my usual two, I am dangerously low on fluids. Everything around me is brown except for black oil oozing from freshly paved road. It's Sunday, so no construction activity, and I traverse a cordoned off lane under full heat of afternoon sun.

There is no place to sit and no shade to duck into. The only living things I see are jack rabbits scurrying among oil rigs, sludge pools, and sorghum fields.

At night when I review my day's events, it boggles my mind when I realize how much awesomeness gets packed into twenty-four hours and just how much of it is unplanned. But on this particular day, even with that consideration, I anticipate an uneventful twenty-five miles into Ackerly. I am wrong.

I must do laundry every ten days or so. You don't want to meet me into my ninth day, though I do my best to disguise my stench with heavy doses of Gold Bond powder. I take full advantage to clean as many items as possible when I have the opportunity. That means I may do my laundry in a rain jacket, pajama bottoms, and flip flops.

That's how I meet Jim.

Jim works at Quick Clean Coin Operated Laundry, and I interview him in all my fancy apparel. He suggests I come back tomorrow to talk with Sandra, the owner. He says she would be a great interview. But I never go back. My days are already full, and I have a schedule to follow. Instead, I continue on.

With only a few unrefreshing hot sips of water left, I do something I've only done once when I was a novice walker in Vermont and never have to do again. I knock on a complete stranger's door—one of only a handful seen all day—to refill my water bottles. Twenty-one miles from the laundromat, Sandra opens the door. She invites me in, fills up my belly with iced water, then fills my bottles.

I promise, I will never take ice for granted again!

Strategically located for a waystation, Sandra's house apparently attracts anyone who needs anything. I'm introduced to her husband, who teaches me a little about cowboying and ranching. That remains of what little I know about cowboying and ranching. I also learn I am only three miles or one hour from Ackerly, less than the two hours I erroneously calculated.

I love when the numbers fall in my favor.

Just as I reach the Ackerly turnoff, a car drives directly at me in the breakdown lane. Angel Rosa Morales has arrived. She saw me walking against traffic—always a good safety rule—as I headed out of Big Spring in the morning and saw me again late in the afternoon as she returned from visiting her daughter in Lamesa, so she turned around to pick me up.

She didn't ask. She told me, "Get in the car." Being close enough to the end of the day, I accept her invitation to drive me to a hotel, different from the one where I had negotiated a reduced rate, but I don't care. My angel came without my calling.

Synchronicities happen faster these days and without conscious awareness. It used to be I had to first hold the intent and watch it grow like the corn that matures from seed to harvest along my route back east. Today, it simply materializes.

October 22, 2015
30.5230°N, 87.9033°W
Fairhope, Alabama

"I just finished the last mile of a long, hot day."

Many of my journal entries begin that way. After the pleasant, flat landscape of the Florida panhandle, I approach my first hill in 250 miles on the western border of Alabama. Topping it, I am slightly annoyed to see another hill and then another. The day's end begins to feel elusive. I eventually near the outskirts of a town, come to a church (there is always a church), and pause.

John de Graaf, coauthor of the highly acclaimed book *Affluenza: The All-Consuming Epidemic*, had directed me to Fairhope for its history and great sense of community. An original member of the town once remarked the Single Tax Colony had a fair hope of succeeding, thus its moniker. An acquaintance of John's was to host me—or so was the idea. We discussed loose plans before I left for the stretch from Jacksonville, but we never reconnected until it was too late. Her schedule had changed, so I was left without a host.

Time to put Plan B into action, which typically involves making new friends in a coffee shop.

I pause and think, *I'm here. Now what? I really could use an angel.*

I feel satisfied and accomplished after the day's vigorous workout, but my body language must say otherwise. Along comes a car screeching into the church parking lot. It stops directly in front of me. Out explodes a lightning bolt of energy of a woman talking into her cell phone—car running, driver's door left open—she walks directly toward me. She looks quite determined as though on a mission. Holding the phone to her chest, she eyes me and asks pointedly, "Do you need a place to stay tonight?"

I have learned not to be too explicit in my silent petitions to angels. Experience suggests that, when I articulate a loosely defined need, what results often turns out far grander than the thing I may have hoped for.

Theresa Lacey is most certainly the answer to my appeal. I do not stay the one night in her home with her family. I stay four!

I later track down Maggie, my intended original host. She was understandably distracted by planning a memorial service for her brother. I suppose her angels guarded her much needed sanctuary while mine sent Theresa in her stead.

Here's how Theresa tells the story. She drove past me as I walked towards town. I was distracted by an attempt to help an injured dog, so she didn't receive the typical friendly wave from me that most cars do. A voice in her head whispered, "Bring her home." According to Theresa, the voice gradually grew louder until it urged so insistently that she turned around in her driveway, pointed her car back towards town center, spotted me at the church, pulled in, and bounded out. She said the troubled look on my face told her everything she needed to know about having made the right decision. Apparently, my exhaustion on the inside looks a lot like distress on the outside.

Still, the voice in her head is astute. I'm glad she has awareness to listen. I therefore get to explore the Alabama Delta without the need to siphon energy towards finding places to sleep or eat.

Such synchronicity has come to define the walk. My sister Pam and I call it PFM: Pure Freakin' Magic. Others who've joined the walk or have experienced long distance travel call it road magic or, if in the wilderness, trail magic. While I do not yet understand the genesis of such moments of kismet, I do welcome them, appreciate them, and work with them.

Several years before GNHUSA was even a thought, I transitioned out of my position as the director of a community social-profit organization in order to start my own consulting business. I knew if I worked as hard on my own venture as I had for others in past jobs, it was sure be a success. I sought counsel from a good friend and life coach, Josephine Romano, to help me through the transition.

Josephine encouraged me to create a vision board to help me visualize what I desired in terms of my new career and life in general. I had heard of vision boards but never felt compelled to make one. Doing the exercise can involve making a rudimentary list of hopes and dreams or a more elaborate project, say a beautiful collage of pictures representing the same—whatever works.

It all sounded pretty foo-foo, like something someone would do to imagine having control over things even if not. But I designed one anyway. Since I can be fairly geeky and serious, rather than craft something worthy of framing, I made a Power-Point and saved it on my computer's desktop in order to absorb its impact every day. I put stuff in those slides that felt absurd at the time, that captured my way-out-of-my-comfort-zone wildest dreams. If I'm really going to do this, why not aim high?

After the walk concluded, I dusted off that vision board when I found it in one of the few stored boxes from my move out of Vermont. Everything I infused into it, every wish I visualized, every outrageous dream captured in bits and bytes came true—all but the ones related to my elder years (I like to think I am not there yet). For example, essentially confined to a Ford station wagon as a young adult, I have since enjoyed travel to places around the globe I would call exotic. Of greater consequence, I have excellent health, a loving family and great friends, and am blessed to have met and received teachings from world renowned spiritual giants—my yesterday, today, and tomorrow sages. Peace Pilgrim featured prominently in my visioning. I couldn't possibly have known how my life would later intersect with the memory of her.

It's time to take this visioning stuff seriously, I admit to myself. A new one is unquestionably in order. This time, post-walk, I'm aiming ever so much higher: I'm shooting for the sparkly stars!

In my third year of walking in Greenville, Florida, Andy's car screeched as he pulled over, coughing up a trail of dust. Shirtless and tattooed, he jumped out of his car excited to share his story of backpacking coast-to-coast with his dog and sailing to twenty-four countries over the course of four years. "We are so much alike," so said that self-proclaimed vagabond, "I'm just out of prison for three and a half years. I've had a lot of time to reflect on things.

"I'm not a religious person by any stretch of the imagination," he continued, "but there is synchronicity in the universe. You have to be with the stars. We are all God. We are all part of a living organism. We may be the eyeball, we may be the eye or the tongue, but we are all a piece of that energy."

So, I work with Pure Freakin' Magic more intentionally, and life has been one surprise after another. Deepak Chopra coined his own word for it, synchrodestiny, when something defies the chaos of the universe and falls into place as if meant to be. Chopra takes the concept further to imply Pure Freakin' Magic *is* meant to be, that synchronicities contain purpose and meaning and have direction and intention.

Once we comprehend concepts informing synchrodestiny, we will "understand nothing less than the dynamics and mechanics of creation itself." As I understand it, that's how vision boards work. You imbue them with intent that calls on creation. When nourished by your dreams, their purpose matures, then materializes. In other words, they are mirrors which point toward the heavens and reflect back to you.

Doesn't that sound like prayer?

Doesn't that feel like the walk?

I love the inherent mystery of it all and am fascinated how science is catching up to such implicit truths. So, I work with it—admittedly, often not so well. But the more I trust my experiences, the greater my application and more synchrodestinies abound.

Some call them miracles, some call them magic, some call them the eyeball of God—I just call them . . . and often.

Things materialize according to my thoughts whether by design or by laziness even when my intentions and attentions are not so pure.

In my early twenties, I kept a running tally of tragedies in my life, including my mother's suicidal ideations, the bomb that killed a young man in my college dorm, the eruption of Mount St. Helens and subsequent quarantine due to a worldwide ash cloud, robbery by knifepoint that ended when my assailant lost a toe by gunshot. Yada, yada, yada. I etched them in my brain in the same penetrating way I had the fifty states in alphabetical order as I silently regurgitated them over and over and over, committing them to memory.

It should be no surprise that I received more of the same. I wore those afflictions like medals on my chest but somehow thought my future would be different—brighter. I am an optimist after all.

No one taught me how the mechanics really work. No one instructed me how to pay attention to what I want and not what I don't want. I didn't understand the dynamics until my introduction to Health Realization, since known as the Three Principles of Universal Mind, Consciousness, and Thought, by my dear friend, renowned author, and one of those who walked with me, Dr. Jack Pransky.

I denied, ridiculed, and dragged my heels into eventually seeing the inside-out nature of my reality. When I finally did, a great big hollow hole in my heart—with me since childhood—suddenly healed. What was going on inside of me was being expressed outside of me.

As within so without, as above so below.

Forever the pragmatist, I needed proof. I tried the philosophy on for size and came to find the more I trusted it, the more it worked for me. Unfortunately, I can be exceedingly stubborn and, therefore, reluctant to trust its efficacy. I always require proof. And I find it—in water . . . and exploratory science.

Like people, not all water is alike.

Years ago, I heard of Dr. Masaru Emoto's experimentation with consciousness and water molecules. Exposed to a variety of emotions through thought, sound, or written word, molecules of water transformed into beautiful geometric patterns for positively-charged emotions or chaotic structures for negatively-charged emotions when viewed under a microscope.

Like people, water reacts to human consciousness.

It is not a huge step for me also to believe that people react to water's consciousness, since it makes up an average of sixty percent of an adult human body.

While Dr. Emoto offers enough initial proof, I continue to explore the field of quantum physics exploding with new scientific discoveries ranging from the observable phenomenon of quantum entanglement which Einstein referred to as "spooky action at a distance" to the nonlocality of space-time to Nobel laureate Max Planck's assertion that consciousness is fundamental to all matter.

So, from the beginning of the walk, whether it is truth or not, whether it is fact or theory, I take to writing loving words on my water bottles and expressing words of gratitude for it whether it is hot or iced—no matter how much weight it adds to my luggage.

It never hurts to show love, even to the seemingly insentient.

September 22, 2015
30.4694°N, 83.6302°W
Greenville, Florida

It's a full month before I reach Fairhope, Alabama, where Theresa will greet me. My back, front, sides, and feet are all soaked with sweat on a humid autumn day. My packs prove heavier with each step. Unlike others who get inspired when they see the finish line—invigorated with an extra boost of energy or creativity—I find my enthusiasm curbs. I can't say why but it does. So I've learned to play games with myself to get me through those last steps of the day, often repetitiously listing the states in alphabetical order.

On this day in Florida, my destination turns out not to be much of a destination at all as I happen upon a gas station, a hardware store/takeout restaurant, and a Dollar Store.

There is always a Dollar Store. It is right down the street from the church.

Famished, I get in line behind a woman at the takeout window of the restaurant/hardware store as I wonder who in their right mind ever thought to combine chili with plumbing. I only hope it isn't a metaphor of some kind. The food smells good, though, and it looks clean enough. I scan the board, decide on my order, and when the woman ahead of me grabs her bags to leave, I step forward.

The window slams shut.

"We're closed."

No, there is no chance I could get you anything, imply the hastily latched shutters and rattling of keys as she locks up what I guess are hot dogs, saws, chicken, hammers, French fries, and screws.

I've lived in Vermont for thirty years and always thought of it as rural. The walk provides me with a newer definition of the word. There's nowhere to go, nowhere to eat, and there are not even any doughnuts at the gas station. There are no houses in sight nor a place to meet any of 817 people who supposedly live here, except . . . the Dollar Store.

I attempt to engage in small talk as I purchase my dinner consisting of a greasy bag of nuts and a simulated fruit energy bar, but to no avail.

No one offers. I don't ask. I'm on my own.

After airing out my aching feet and caring for my left ankle, which I'm still nursing after a bad sprain I received ten months ago on the walk, I eat a few nuts, strap on my packs, and keep on moving. It's a seven-hour walk to the next town.

I'll hitch and make these miles tomorrow.

Seven miles later, my thumb still out in the Upper Aucilla Conservation Area near the Jefferson Correctional Institute in Monticello, I get a lift from a Vermonter. His hitch leads me quickly to another, so I am spared thirteen additional miles on top of an already long day of twenty-six. Patrick, a twenty-something year-old black man (and I purposely mention skin color here), operates the second car. After stopping to offer me a ride, he stares at me suspiciously through the passenger's side window and asks, "You're not going to shoot me, are you?"

That's the first time I realize I am the one who needs to be trusted, not solely the other way around. How had I been so blind to the mutual trust that buttresses the bedrock of my days making each moment and every mile possible?

Patrick kindly takes me to the beautiful town center of Monticello, where my lodging options are abundant, or so I think. After we share a real meal, not nuts and bars, I begin to inquire about a room as I move from one pastel-colored bed and breakfast to another.

Camping is still sixteen hundred miles away.

Apparently, Monticello is a stopover for touring bicyclists, and there's "no room at the inn." I find myself randomly wandering magnolia-lined back streets before I decide to cross the main road towards another group of B&Bs when I see Ms. June. Ms. June, mentioned earlier, and I have spoken by phone, though we have yet to meet.

I know it's her I see because, to the surprise of both of us, at the very moment she pulls over, Shanna pulls up right behind her.

Shanna Parker Boutwell and I met recently over pickled pears and spaghetti casserole at the home of Ms. Zelda, seventy miles east in Mayo. Ms. Zelda is the mother-in-law of a host I met in Georgia and a distant relative of Shanna.

And here we are—Ms. June, Shanna, and me—all three of us converging on the same spot at the same moment in a town where none of us lives nor were expected to be.

Shanna asked Ms. June to assist me with finding a host upon my arrival in Monticello, which wasn't supposed to be until tomorrow. Ms. June parked her mammoth Monte Carlo in front of Daffodale House to secure me a night's lodging, which, since I'm here a day early, turns into two nights. She and her amiable second husband, Leroy, generously donate my accommodations.

"Just don't stay in the green room," she warns. "It's haunted."

I have since come to learn the quaint and well-manicured vacationland of Monticello is best known as one of the South's most haunted small towns. The US Chamber of Commerce says one in every three of its historic buildings is thought to be inhabited by ghosts.

The green room it is!

The walls are painted green, but one might more accurately call it the safari room. Decorated with antique African art and leopard print accessories, it boasts strange ghostly music, lights that inexplicably switch on and off, and an occasional woman dressed in white. Though she does not appear to me, admittedly I give in to the spookiness and implore her throughout the night to please allow me to sleep and use the bathroom in private without the worry of eyes on me.

That's hard to do with all the masks, stuffed animals, and spirits crowding my personal space.

Ghosts aside, how uncanny that the three of us happen upon one another just when I so need a kind face and a place to rest my head. Kismet, Pure Freakin' Magic, synchrodestiny, angels . . . no matter what you call it, it works for me, and I suggest you try it, too.

Visioning, I mean.

And, yes, the green room, too.

I continue to let-go-and-let-God, but for me that looks a lot like let-go-and-let-PFM-happen. I like to think magic defines life when I get out of its way. I nevertheless look for empirical proof as PFM follows me all the way around the country until I witness enough extraordinary happenings to assert to myself—this is the way of life.

I will go on to meet people who shatter the concept of what is possible, people unconfined by what has been and have, instead, set into motion what can be—every one of them endowed with one common trait. Humility.

Though rain had long since ceased,
Mr. Ernie and Paula wear rain gear after a 5.69-mile run in
Lavonia, Louisiana, on
November 21, 2015, at 2,398 miles during
Leg 7 of the Happiness Walk.

ENTANGLED ROOTS

Be an example of the absolute perfection you were born into:
unconditional love.

-Michael Galardi aka Jolly
Point Mugu State Park, California

"How many shoes have you gone through?" is the most frequent question people ask me. I find it a bit peculiar that so many people are sincerely interested in the adornments of my feet. Perhaps it's just the easiest way for people to wrap their heads around what I've just told them: "I've walked here from Vermont."

Possibly most people don't hear what I've said—like Native Americans who literally couldn't see the first ships sailing into their harbors because their minds could not adjust to the idea that anything of such magnitude could float on the ocean. In fact, if I instead say, "I've just walked all day from two towns east," most hearers react with astonishment. Eyes pop and jaws drop. But walking five hundred, a thousand, seven thousand, or more miles gets a blank stare and an "Oh, okay."

Pause.

"How many shoes have you gone through?"

The answer is, I've worn through eighteen pairs of running shoes, approximately a new pair every five hundred or so miles, the equivalent to a full rack at a sporting goods store. My feet announce when I need a new pair. My pace may not slow, but my legs and toes forgive nothing at the end of the day. I don't always have an expedient way to find replacement sneakers, so I often find myself walking in pain on six-hundred-mile-old treads past lumberyards, cottonfields, and storage piles of sugar beets.

I become obsessed with finding a shoe store. Finding a store with the right kind of shoe? Well, that's equivalent to finding the holy grail.

"Why are you walking?" people also ask. Their emphasis is not on the "Why?" or the purpose of the walk but rather on the choice to walk as a means of transporting myself around the country. They go on to suggest bicycling as an excellent medium for covering ground or relay stories of people traveling by horse-back, buggy, and even a lawn mower.

"Perhaps you should consider those."

For some reason, they almost never suggest the obvious, a car. Nor do they advise a motorcycle to transit the country as my great uncle Edgar Jones did in 1924 while towing his friend Edward Carter along in his sidecar. Apparently, my adventurous spirit is inherited.

No, those who wonder why I'm walking understand my interest in moving slowly—just not as slowly as I am moving.

And it never crosses people's minds to suggest I run. Perhaps that's because most women my age are grandmothers, so they aren't sure I could survive. In my case, they would be correct, but not necessarily correct for many grandmothers or grandfathers I know.

Curiously enough, I am personally acquainted with two men older than I who ran across the continent. One, the legendary

Newton Baker, makes his home in my hometown of Montpelier, Vermont. In 2015 and at age 73, that survivor of cancer ran the equivalent of 117 back-to-back marathons across the United States in four and a half months with the goal of sparking a much needed renaissance in childhood health and fitness.

Before and after his run, Newton generously shared his on-the-road lessons and offered guidance on my routes and lodging. We had hoped to cross paths in Texas, but he made much greater headway than I could manage. He celebrated with me when I reached my ten thousand miles in Vermont, though, and he remains a true inspiration.

Through a network of roots, Newton introduces me to Mr. Ernie, with whom I do get to rendezvous in Louisiana.

November 21, 2015
30.5591°N, 91.5559°W
Livonia, Louisiana

"We are all here just walking each other home" goes another saying of the Bluebirds, the joy-filled group I met in Lafayette, Louisiana. While most of us walk, some of us run. I relate to the former while Ernest Andrus qualifies as one of the latter.

Mr. Ernie holds counsel over biscuits and gravy with his fan base of the day. His police escorts return to their normal duties after assuring his safe passage along Highway 190 from Lo-Vac's parking lot in Lottie, Louisiana, to the C-Store and Grill in Livonia 5.69 miles to the east while, waving a small Old Glory, and chatting about vintage motorcars.

A 92-year-old WWII Navy veteran, Mr. Ernie is on his first cross-continental run. He doesn't know it yet, but he will conclude his itinerary from San Diego to the Atlantic Ocean in 999 hours, an angel sign, on his 93rd birthday among an enthusiastic group of supporters cheering "Run, Ernie! Run!" He will then return home, determine a sedentary life is not his speed, and start again, running west from Georgia at age 95 with a goal of reaching California by the age of 100. Though a foot ailment keeps him from dipping his toes into the Pacific Ocean, he makes respectable headway and ends his enterprise in Texas one-third of the way home. He authorizes a proxy, John Martin, to complete the run in his stead.

For now, Mr. Ernie, Mel and Sybil Comeaux (his hosts of Krotz Springs), Marvin Cooper (my ride), and I squeeze into a booth at Penny's Diner in Livonia, Louisiana. The three of us who ran are still damp after a morning that started with hard rain. Marvin had made an advance run to a nearby store and purchased each of us paper-thin yellow ponchos. Just as we pulled them over our drenched heads, the sun shone through.

"The day which the Lord hath made," Mr. Ernie brands this holy act. I've welcomed many of such inspired days, myself.

Marvin is a new acquaintance. We met two weeks before and, like many generous people, he offered to find me a host in Baton Rouge. "Did I need anything else?" he inquired. And that is how a walker found her way to Lottie so she could run with an icon of a man, her now idol and dear friend, Ernest.

Mr. Ernie consults his GPS, collects our names, lends us each an 18-inch American flag on a stick, and checks to make sure he has his phone, his wallet, and his teeth. He clicks his stopwatch, and off we go at a 28-minute-per-mile clip. As runners #701 and #702, we feel honored to enjoy his stories and partake for the next three hours in his record-breaking enterprise.

More than six feet tall, Mr. Ernie's bones have submitted to the gravity of his years. His gravy-filled potbelly spills over his fire-truck red elastic jogging shorts complementing the rainbow spiral of his tie-dyed t-shirt. Keeping the morning's sweat from his eyes, he wears a rainbow headband that matches his shirt.

Compression socks worn for circulation kiss his tanned bony knees, and his smile shines all the way to the county line.

He's just like Forrest Gump, one might say—and they do say! In fact, between runs, Mr. Ernie will later run with me right onto Santa Monica Pier, a very Forrest-Gump-like moment for the two of us to share together.

On the Happiness Walk— mile by mile and interview by interview—I slowly make my way from state to state. Mr. Ernie runs to make distance at an even slower pace but with so much more pizzazz. "The more runners, the more fun. You walk, I run," he posts on his Facebook page. "If you see me on the highway, wave, shout, honk. It keeps me moving."

Like Newton and me, Ernie crosses the country with a particular cause in mind. Mr. Ernie's goal is to raise enough money to return a Landing Ship Tank he helped restore, the USS LST 325, to Normandy, France for the 75th D-Day Memorial Service in 2019. Though the date has passed and his feet have stopped, his fundraising efforts have not. Like Newton Baker, he is not one to easily succumb to de-feet!

I now enjoy a special bond with people identifying as long-distance anything across Turtle Island, as Native Americans so appropriately called our American continent. I feel as though I've joined a unique, not too terribly small, but distinguished club with whose members I have a sense of fellowship. We appreciate one another's stories, trials, and joys, our highs and lows, and most definitely, our accomplishments. I've learned few folks outside our finite group can truly grasp the essence of a long walk or the agony of having finished one. To my fellow wanderers, I wave, I shout, and I trumpet my metaphoric horn in admiration of your belief in yourself.

It seems all people want to be in a clan of some kind. It probably isn't shocking news that Happiness Walk interviews reveal people most value our social connectedness. We all want to give love and receive love. We all want to feel a sense of belonging.

"But for me," says Toni Bankston of Baton Rouge, Louisiana, "it's bigger than that. It's the need to love a lot of people." Toni calls it Big Love—where you reach out of your immediate circle and love beyond measure.

When I was a poor student at Boston University, I sometimes had an extra fifty cents to my name at the end of the week. Twenty-five cents might buy me a freshly baked bagel with cream cheese as reprieve from the unremarkable cafeteria food I consumed daily. I used the remaining quarter to purchase a round-trip ride on the Blue Line on the subway—locally known as the T—into Logan Airport.

Back then, everyone had access to the airline gates, so I would find myself a well-positioned seat and watch loving reunions take place as people disembarked and found their people. It gave me a sense of hope to see such open displays of love, and it alleviated my tendencies towards loneliness at the time.

It's easy to be invisible in a large city.

I revisit such feelings in Ridgeway, Wisconsin, on August 13, 2019. There isn't much but farmland between my morning and evening when I come across that tiny village. The only establishment where one could get some food is the local bar. Tuesday night at The Wheel is Euchre night. Half the town must have come out for the big card game. I am immediately accepted into the fold when someone shouts from across the bar. "You must be the one they were talking about on the ham radio today. They said there was a lady walking in the rain on Route 151 and that she must have something mentally wrong with her."

It's hard to be invisible in a small town.

Everyone enjoys the anecdote, especially me. We all laugh, and the loud one buys me dinner and a drink. My options are minimal, which suits me just fine, as I get incapacitated by too many choices. My life has become simple and exceedingly uncomplicated.

Established as a welcomed guest, I watch with great interest as tables of four are hastily spread across the floor and partners are randomly chosen from an old milk bucket. I cannot figure out the rules, but the cajoling, changing of chairs, hugs, and handshakes make for a fascinating and engaging evening as a community of friends shows Big Love in spades—and clubs, diamonds, and hearts.

Both my appetite and loneliness assuaged, I camp across the street under the large pavilion built to accommodate the entire town. While I am happy to have made new friends, the retreat into my tent affords me comfort I no longer find in someone else's home nor on a down-covered bed. Like Freddie, I have come to prefer the familiarity of the floor.

Communing with one another—that's what we are here to do, or at least hope to do. Some of us walk with one another, some of us run, and some of us need more communing than others.

November 15, 2014
36.6777°N, 76.9225°W
Franklin, Virginia

I am well into my second pair of walking shoes and about to reach a major milestone. I arrived in New York City two years before, and I've long since attained the goal of reaching Washington, DC.

I juggle my work and family schedules to return to the road in Virginia. As far as I can see, there isn't much around—just more of the same long road lined with loblolly pines and cotton fields.

Mr. Marcus, a taxi driver I met a couple days back, will drop off my backpack at my day's destination. He tells of his time in prison and of crimes of which he repents. He surely must make up for some of his past transgressions with the many kindnesses he bestows upon me. Beyond transporting gear, providing rides to and from starting and ending points along with several safety check-ins over several days, and garnering interviews for me with the county newspaper, Mr. Marcus introduces me to many of the locals.

One such local is his once professional football-player friend, Greg Scott, who founded a nonprofit comprised of coaching, mentoring, feeding, and community service program, Cover 3 Foundation, for youth in his hometown of Franklin and surrounding counties. I catch the tail end of a youth football game attended by what seems to be every parent in southeast Virginia. The uniforms are colorful, the cheers are encouraging, and the camaraderie is optimal (which, of course, is the point).

I don't think Mr. Marcus smiles. His look is stern accompanied by a sideways tilt of his head and lowered brows. It's as if his heart says one thing but his face, trained in a prison cell, says, "Don't mess with me." He's cloaked in a hopeful vision of himself, though. His personal social media tag line reads, "I AM the CORNERSTONE that was rejected by the builders, but I AM the most important STONE." I'm unsure if he refers directly to himself or a higher being. I believe Mr. Marcus does not precisely distinguish himself from a higher being.

He sends me messages for several years to come. His latest one reads, "May the Creator of Time and Space be the Light that continues to bring comfort to your being. Love Ya!!!!" He sends that salutation from behind bars. Sadly, Mr. Marcus seems to have retreated to his comfort zone—not yet unshackled from life's temptations. Unthwarted by his circumstance, he repents and prays—and sends microbursts of love via Instagram.

I sincerely hope the children in his friend Greg's program, which teaches self-control and self-discipline, will build a solid foundation for making choices leading to strong relationships and sustained happiness. The choices we make every day can either glue us to a positive trajectory or a less desirable one. But as in the example of my friend Mr. Marcus, that path is malleable. With your back to the radiance of life, you will see only your shadow. Each moment is a new opportunity to choose your orientation, to face darkness or light.

Maybe becoming unglued isn't always a bad thing.

There was a time when I once groped around in the dark—in college, in particular, when the void in my heart was ultimately cemented in loneliness. But I love the sun on my face and don't miss the shackles of my misguided self drawing me into choices I will later regret.

October 12, 2019
42.4440°N, 76.5019°W
Ithaca, New York

I claim my six-inch thick plastic-wrapped mat, a blue plastic wrapped pillow, and a set of sheets offered me by St. John Rescue Mission staff. I don't know exactly where I am. No one on the forty-minute bus drive from Ithaca asks. We each seek shelter from the extreme cold that arrives weeks before the downtown shelter is planned to open, so arrangements are made to house us at a "local" church.

I have exhausted all other options and called upon the police for assistance. "Do you know of a safe place for me to set up my tent?" I ask a police officer in hopes he will lend me a slice of the station's lawn—another suggestion I learned from Biker Chic Nic.

"There's a homeless shelter just down the street. Let me call and make arrangements."

I am a good example of the multitude of reasons someone finds themself in a homeless shelter. I'm not exactly homeless— just houseless, but there are no hotel options, and the police prefer me off the streets, so I end up somewhere forty miles away from Ithaca on the basketball-court floor of a church, where I will sleep on a portable plastic mattress provided for me as I share the warm haven with several others and feel spoiled by glistening multi-stalled bathroom facilities.

I put a great degree of trust into the St John's staff. After so long on the road, I cringe at completely giving over my control—something I suspect my floormates are accustomed to.

There's also a pile of paperwork totaling twenty different forms. I am flummoxed as to what to put down as my address. As someone who worked with social services and nonprofit organizations, I understand the protections and data collection driving such processes, so I am both annoyed and appreciative at the same time.

A Harvard longitudinal study on happiness concludes that "the good life is built on strong relationships" and that "happiness is love—full stop." I wonder how people establish such relationships when they, like some of those with whom I share the parquet floor, are transient and long for people to look into their eyes though they have no Euchre group or running partners or football team to call their tribe.

When I meander through an aspen grove in Utah, I do so with purpose. I heard of the network of underground roots that connects trees to each other, and how each trunk, though appearing separate to the unknowing eye, shares an exact genetic makeup with each and all of the others. While one tree can live up to 150 years, the collective may be as ancient at 80,000 years. Each tree sustains the other, protects its sibling, assimilates its decaying carcass, and apportions its nutriments to where they're needed most in a natural display of harmony, oneness, and community.

As I travel, I am tapping into my roots . . . I am tapping into Big Love.

When I began the Happiness Walk, I banked each mile I racked up like pennies strewn on the ground. Ka-ching. Ka-ching. One hundred miles—done! One state—accomplished! New England—Ka-ching!

The Northeast is deceiving. The further I got from home, the longer it took to wrap up a state, and I quickly stopped measuring my bounty in hundreds of miles but rather in wads of one thousand.

Though I continue to measure my distances as I move more deeply around the country, it's the experiences I put in my pocket along with the feathers and stones that mark a successful journey. They are the tree trunks in my grove that account for my riches.

I know I am rewiring my brain with every step I take, and goodness knows I need it. It's what my body cries out for, my mind seeks, and my inner being desires. All the eventual eighteen pairs of shoes I wear on the Happiness Walk help me achieve what I once considered unthinkable. Each breath offers me the impulse to live it fully, and every day I am grateful I still have miles before me—and my wallet, my GPS, and my teeth.

Before I finish walking, I will walk in McKinleyville, California, past the world's tallest totem carved from a single log; under the world's widest freeway in Houston, Texas; past the world's smallest police station in Carrabelle, Florida; into the smallest church in America, in Townsend, Georgia, and; by the world's smallest diner in Watkins Glen, New York.

I will see the tallest shovel in Creedmore, Texas, and largest wooden old-fashioned telephone in Roggen, Colorado. I will never set eyes on the tallest tree at its undisclosed location in Redwood National Park but will walk through a connected grove of aspen trees.

I will eat in the frog and mozzarella capitals of the world (I do not indulge in frog but love the cheese) and in the venue of the first world championship bare-knuckle heavyweight prize fight in Kenner, Louisiana. I will drink in the first establishment since Prohibition in San Francisco, California, a place that sparked the revolution in the craft brewing industry.

If such roadside attractions don't make you want to go on your own pilgrimage, perhaps the thought of reaching out beyond your immediate circle to expand your tribe to the likes of Mr. Ernie, Mr. Marcus, and my St. John's companions and Euchre buddies will.

That we can envision and build such unusual markers along our highways and byways provides remarkable entertainment. That we can build long tunnels through mountains and land probes on an asteroid defines the concept of phenomenal. Why aren't we as imaginative and willing to build vital communities that cultivate strong bonds with one another? Why do we allow homelessness and loneliness to flood our streets? How unfathomable and—in my humble opinion—reprehensible are such human-caused conditions. If we most value our social connections, what keeps us from embracing the Big Love of aspens?

While my curiosity remains unsatisfied with regard to those disheartening questions, I do gain insights to other life mysteries at the navel of Buddha—just beyond hell.

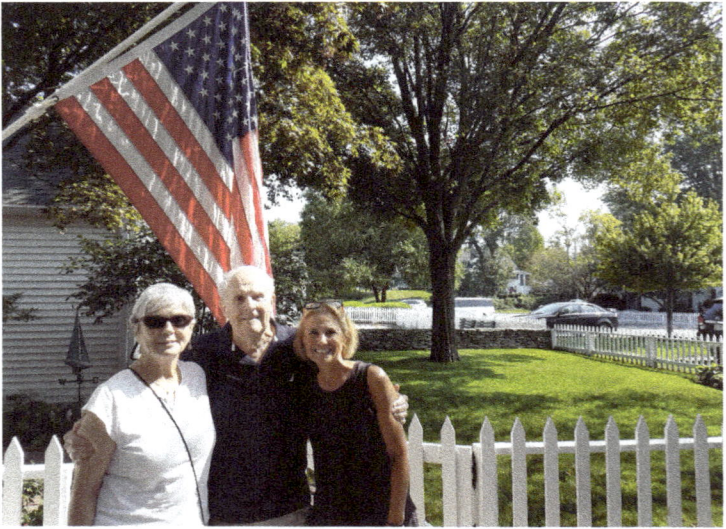

US Army Lieutenant Colonel Harlan Chapman shared war stories during Paula's visit with him and his wife, Fran, left, in Vermilion, Ohio. Alexandra Delis-Abrams of Idaho, a supporter of the Happiness Walk, introduced Paula to her nephew's wife, Dana Corogin, who hosted Paula in Ohio and arranged an interview with Lieutenant Colonel Chapman on September 20, 2019, at 9,153 miles during Leg 16 of the Happiness Walk.

I'M A BELIEVER

The true essence of everyone exists; it's just hidden in multiple layers of conditioning that we've been exposed to. And taking the time to undo those conditioned layers will yield a phenomenal feeling of the joy of what it's like to be in form.

—Harry Uvegi
New York City

The twenty-foot golden statue rests peacefully on its side, right arm tucked under its head with the other arm draped along the ridges of its reclining left side. I sit cross-legged at the navel of Siddhārtha Gautama's likeness in the Parinirvana Stupa: a sacred site in Kushinagar, India, honoring the occasion of Lord Buddha's passage from this life.

I try to stay reverent but am distracted by several bug bites courtesy of the city of Patna on this day in 2013, although I am the least distressed of my fourteen-member tour group. We have been praying since Varanasi, India, during a bus trip of some two hundred miles (measured in India as kilometers, of course) to receive the blessings of Buddhist texts by visiting revered landmarks: to awaken us to the great gifts of enlightenment.

Unsuspectingly those gifts come for several people in the guise of a great awakening of the bowels. Maybe it was the soup broth of last night's dinner, the dung on the walls used for insulation, or the omnipresent ditches used for toilets on the sides of the dirt roads. Possibilities are endless, but so are the pharmaceuticals tucked into our overstuffed fanny packs along with bug spray, sunscreen, and prayer malas. Patna is not a worse hell than what we've seen so far—as we were told to expect—just a bigger one.

Those of us able to sit in meditation without intense stomach rumblings find ourselves jolted from our contemplative state by the stirrings of a six-year-old boy who charges into the temple, aims his plastic gun at the reclining Buddha, and shouts: "Ka-pow, ka-pow, you're dead!"

This is not how I envisioned a pilgrimage. But expectations prove bewildering beasts. Rarely are the things I want the things I receive—or value.

Death is certain. Our time of death is uncertain. So taught Shakyamuni Buddha according to our American tour guide Amy Miller, Buddhist nun and author of *Buddhism in a Nutshell*. We live in a mortal world with an undetermined lifespan, yet most of the people I know are uncomfortable talking about death or, alternatively, don't give it much consideration. I always find it strange, since—of all the experiences we can have on this Earth—there is only one thing we can count on: an exit—a transition out of this thing we call life.

We can find exceptions to the reluctant, of course. "I'm very ready to go," says Brenda at the Truck Farm Tavern in Almedia, Louisiana. "If everybody felt like me, it would be a wonderful place, but we know that ain't gonna happen."

She explains. "Happiness is not going to be found on this Earth. It's not in religion, church attendance, or in rules or regulations. It's only in him who gives us new life. Satan is the prince and ruler of the power of the air and this is his turf, this is his place." Brenda can't wait to die and leave this living hell to Satan.

It causes her further angst when people don't share her desire with the same amount of fervor, so she refers to her tavern customers as the dead.

"We're born with a dead spirit, so I love on dead people all day long," she asserts. Brenda goes on to serve her customers biscuits and gravy with a double side of bacon washed down with three cups of chicory coffee.

Perhaps they do have a death wish after all.

I spend a lot of time talking about death on the Happiness Walk. An awareness of what awaits us—and its certain visitation upon us—can act as a catalyst to live our lives to the fullest, to appreciate each day, to be thankful for each inhalation that guarantees life until the subsequent exhalation, and for each morning one awakens to brush and floss one's teeth.

In Kushinagar, when I open my eyes, I put my left foot on the floor of my hotel room and say thank you for the gift of life. My right foot meets its partner, and again, I say "Thank you." The arrival of a new day is never guaranteed. Just ask the Bluebirds.

I stretch my sleepy legs and make myself a cup of instant Nescafe. It seems my fervent prayers haven't yet materialized a strong cup of French roast coffee. Since questionable broth will surely replace a satisfying plate of biscuits and gravy on the breakfast menu, I keep my rumblings to a minimum, stick to my imperfect beverage, and minister, instead, to my spiritual hunger.

February 26, 2016
29.7604°N, 95.3698°W
Houston, Texas

I am in a Houston Starbucks when I meet Evil Steve. I would love to tell you how he got his name, but unfortunately the story never got told in my presence. I suspect it's based on the life he led prior to a life-changing accident. A crane he operated tipped over and left him buried alive for six hours beneath rubble. He tells of rebar piercing his heart and of multiple bones broken throughout his body. Despite the odds, there he is sitting next to me drinking a four-dollar latte.

Self-proclaimed rabble-rouser, bully, and drunken homophobe, Steve expected to be paralyzed should he actually survive. He faced probable death with anger and bitterness, feeling a victim to his bad fortune. Then one night, he had a dream. He remembers the date clearly. In his dream, all the people he knew visited him and, as if watching a movie, he observed interactions with each of them. His dream revealed hard truths concerning every one of his relationships.

He woke up suddenly and cried aloud, "How dare I?"

That became his personal mantra from that moment on. And from that moment on, all his motivations turned on their head.

In his exchange with me, Evil Steve does not live up to his name. He is kind and generous and humble, and I shall not call him evil anymore. I suspect his epiphany transformed him so that he dare not forget, as he tells me, that everyone has a story and we may never know what that story is. So he chooses to think of others' needs over his own.

He buys me a grande coffee and, knowing that he and I are from the same grove of aspens connected by our entangled roots, shows genuine interest in my life. As a monk who interrupted my intense prayer at India's Bodhgaya Stupa so simply and succinctly whispered as he gently stroked my emotional pain he could somehow see, "There's more than one way."

Steve's story is consistent with recorded near-death experiences of people who report traveling through a tunnel of light before reuniting with loving family on the other side. Though Steve didn't depict the same thing, he described a classic life-review scenario. I often wonder how differently I would live my life if everyone I ever encountered became my truth-teller at some unknown, but guaranteed, future date.

Somewhat like Brenda, Buddhists find themselves motivated to think upon death five times per day, perhaps for the same reason she does. I'm sure there must be many benefits to such a practice, but Steve's and others' witness to an accountable afterlife is the only one I need.

Steve's is not the first nor last near-death account I hear as I walk and interview. It's not even the only story about being buried alive nor of returning to life after apparent death.

Clearly, we are resilient beings. Undoubtedly, something greater is at play here, greater than my head can grasp, but luckily not too great for my heart nor my soul.

"Are you a believer?" I am asked for the umpteenth time as I venture below the Mason-Dixon line.

When I first hear it, the question catches me off guard. It feels as intrusive as a home invasion to the reserved northerner I am. I've come, however, to accept the question as part of a normal southern greeting along with "Can you make a roux?"

My religious orientation seems to be on everyone's mind south of the mid Atlantic. But I can't agree to the homogenization of our diverse spiritual convictions—that to be a believer means only one thing, having a personal relationship with Jesus Christ. I don't mean it in a derogatory way, not at all. I believe Jesus is one of our greatest spiritual teachers. But beliefs, as expressed to me by so many, come in many sizes, shapes, and dimensions. Who is to say one path is any better than the other? Unlike Brenda, I don't subscribe to the idea that our individual spirit can ever be dead, so I continue to walk in joy along the path of my own choosing.

While belief in an Infinite Creator gives purpose to my life and provides perspective and peace during times of pain, chaos, and confusion, understanding my spiritual nature means so much more than that. Seeking my truth allows me to be conscious in ways that do not require that I have an intermediary. And in that, I am a true believer.

"Everyone who seeks, finds. And to everyone who knocks, the door will be open," said Christ. Perhaps he might also add, "There's more than one path to the door."

When I get to Hawaii, I learn the path to the door José travels is different from most.

January 9, 2018
21.3069°N, 157.8583°W
Honolulu, Hawaii

I meet José at Diamond Head Beach Park in Honolulu. "I like just to be happy and that's all. I retire already so I don't want to work hard no more. Just like to enjoy what I have now and then waiting for Jesus. When Jesus comes, I want to go to heaven."

A self-identified cartel assassin, José refused a reprehensible assignment, even for him—details I will not divulge. He tells of a time at Peniel P'ni El Pearl Gates Pentecostal Church in Pearl City, Hawaii, where he prayed and surrendered his full self to the Lord before he fainted to the floor. He shook and cried as if in the throes of a seizure.

Before him appeared an apparition, a large being with long wavy hair. The being, dressed in white, brandished a mighty sword. The same being appeared again at three o'clock the next morning.

"I fought for you. You are safe now." Thus did José perceive the being's message. The following Sunday, without knowledge of José's visitation, his pastor preached about a fifteen-foot celestial warrior, Archangel Michael. José's warrior. He brings news that even a hired assassin and Starbuck's Steve can find new purpose and peace.

At the time of José's telling, I had no idea I, too, would meet Archangel Michael. He does not come to me in a dream. Instead, we meet as he vacations in Michigan.

September 10, 2019
location undisclosed

Archangel Michael rolls his own cigarettes, drinks Genesee beer, and sports dreadlocks underneath a knitted gray skullcap. He tells of his immaculate conception, his distaste for "dumbed-down humans," and of an imminent war against Lucifer anticipated on American soil—Brenda's hell.

"Shit is going down," he proclaims. "The best you can do is don't stand down." His brilliant smile casts a shadow on the sun, although he offers his ultimately optimistic message, "Good will prevail," and he shares his advice to us simple humans, "Never doubt yourself."

And so the question remains. Am I a believer?

I answer yes. Yes, because I have searched, studied, questioned, and adjusted my views over decades of my life, and I suspect I will adjust, tinker, and modify them further as I open myself to flowering epiphanies much like a pure lotus transcending muddy waters to blossom in the light.

I answer yes because I have been guided by so many road angels, dragonflies, and even a fictitious Forrest Gump on this walkabout.

And I say yes because I've met an archangel and didn't have to die to do so.

So, while we sit with our own understandings of messages from Buddha and Jesus and other enlightened beings, I can actually empathize with waitress Brenda's point of view, especially if one believes the beautiful anecdotes of people who've died only to come back to life, which I do.

Dannion Brinkley, whose story I've had the privilege of hearing, died four times and was brought back to life each occasion. In his book *Saved by the Light,* he claims he was clinically dead for twenty-eight minutes. Not once did he witness a hell, and according to him, he would have been a good candidate for fire and brimstone. Stories of the afterlife as reported by Dannion, Steve, and others sound glorious. Unlike some people, however, I'm not in any rush to experience it even though I've long since dropped any fear of doing so.

Yes, life is full of suffering. That is one of Buddhism's Four Noble Truths. Luckily, there are three others. One—there is a cause for suffering; it takes self-reflection and honesty with oneself, but the causes are not too difficult to see, particularly if you believe in multiple lives. Two—there is an end to suffering that's harder to see, but good to know. And three—there is a path to the end of suffering that holds promise for getting us out of our misery. The task left to us is to see that things go awry for reasons we may not understand, believe that life is meant to be joyful, and discover our own course to heaven on Earth.

I'm told Archangel Michael is on it!

Again, according to the monk under the Bodhi Tree, "There's more than one way."

Figuring that out is what I'm attempting to do on my trip to South Asia. I'm still in the midst of great conflict over my marriage. It's the first time I've traveled by myself to a distant and unfamiliar country. As I sit on the tarmac in Boston anticipating liftoff of the British Airways flight to New Delhi in 2013, I already feel ungrounded. I can't identify the source of the pit in my belly nor of the tears that stream down my face.

I don't know why I'm doing this. Why am I doing this? I silently repeat to myself.

But, of course I know. I've been stuck between fear and loneliness for too many years. I can no longer accept the slow death of my soul that keeps pace with the slow death of my marriage. I need to break out of my slumber and find answers to life's age-old inquiries: Who am I? What is my purpose here? Who or what is God? But while I embark on a solitary seeking of wisdom on a solo trip, I know I'm not entirely alone. I have the safety of a tour group led by my Vermont friend Venerable Amy waiting for me seven thousand miles away—and I have my faith.

Strapped into my aisle seat, I clutch a book aptly titled *Solo* by Kwame Alexander and loaned to me by my friend Carol Maloney who joined me in Savannah. It's an account of a hero's journey about finding oneself. I sense I will find something significant ahead of me just as I know I am leaving something significant behind. But I really don't want to find myself. I want to recreate myself. Who do I want to become? Will I experience my own heroine's journey? And will the ancient secrets of India, Nepal, and Bhutan hold answers in their sacred chambers?

"Please allow this pilgrimage to be the beginning of the end to my suffering," I quietly pray to Buddha as he is getting shot by that cheeky six-year-old. "Please, please, please show me Truths 2, 3, and, especially, 4!"

The temples do not disappoint nor do the caves, hilltops, stupas, nor monasteries. Even though crowds are omnipresent, somehow, we manage to navigate narrow passageways, assemble our group alone at crowded tourist sites, and get invited into the bowels of non-tourist sacred spaces. We meet many high-level geshes and have the unbelievable good karma to meet Tulku Tenzin Phuntsok Rinpoche: a ten-year-old at the time who was featured in the documentary *Unmistaken Child* as the reincarnation of a renowned Tibetan lama. Two of our group, one other seeker and me, spend an overnight under the treasured Bodhi Fig Tree where Buddha purportedly attained enlightenment.

I pray. I recite mantras. I prostrate. I circumnavigate the temple endless times.

I plead, I beg, and I appeal for guidance and direction.

Needless to say, after all my incessant groveling and knee bruising prostrations, I don't achieve the enlightened state attained by Buddha, though I am keenly aware I am moving further down my chosen path. It is an experience I will carry with me forever—that and a couple of fallen fig leaves.

My karma continues into Bhutan, birthplace of Gross National Happiness, where I visit on my own after saying goodbye in Nepal to my tour friends. My trip to Asia constitutes the kindergarten run to my eventual graduation of walking alone around the United States, which will require several gradual steps and two fateful pushes. But however incredible my first solo journey, not all is fine and dandy in South Asia, just as not all is fine and dandy on my walk. And I don't refer to the gastronomic challenges.

I come upon a police presence in Kathmandu, Nepal, at the Boudhanath Stupa—the iconic one with the beautifully painted eyes. I learn that moments before, a monk set himself on fire, the hundredth Tibetan to self-immolate as a political protest against Chinese policies in his homeland. One does not hope to experience such a local practice on tour, but I sense I needed to witness the plight of anguished Tibetans and acknowledge their pain.

Through systematic acts of domination, we—the collective—have created a void in our wisdom cultures by whitewashing the rich traditions and native ways of indigenous and other peoples around the globe. Exterminating languages, ceremonies, and ancestral and cosmic connections accelerates loss and movement into the shadows, forcing generations of peoples into spiritual and cyclical poverty. Since our roots are connected, the fact impoverishes us all.

I believe we must acknowledge suffering, not avoid recognizing it, for such things give testimony to what we don't want. Adversity can inform and act as a guide. It can also destroy you if you wear it too long. Instead, we are counseled not to attach ourselves to life's untoward conditions but rather to use them as catalysts to create something different, something better.

The lessons about suffering assault me time and time again on the Happiness Walk, and I am routinely unhappy in the process of my schooling. I suspect some of my empathic walking partners also get overwhelmed by their own shadows and that their discomfort deepens when they regularly witness the suffering of others. I try to use such moments to learn my Buddhist lessons. In return, I hope I'm also able to transmute some of the pain people share through the simple act of listening and by acknowledging the worth of each person within my circle of influence.

When I head back to Vermont from Bhutan, I'm full to the brim with new experiences, thoughts, epiphanies, and plans. The esoteric side of me contemplates an altered version of my life's purpose, and my practical side just can't wait to flush toilet paper down a modern toilet.

I really don't have a clue about the bushes and open pavement ahead of me.

March 20, 2018
International Day of Happiness
41.0593°N, 124.1431°W
Trinidad, California

As I make my way north of Trinidad, California, away from the brambles and beach back into the welcomed traffic on US 101, I carry a small stone surely intentionally placed for me for when I opened my eyes, having slid 108 feet down a rocky, muddy chute to receding ocean waters. The one-inch stone is not a translucent agate as I had hoped to find on the northern California beach but a rather muddled and opaque dark green. Still, I cherish it.

My hands shake as I pluck the stone from the sand. Through my tears of relief, I see a thin line of silica down the length of its oblong shape, ostensibly cutting the stone in half. Fifty-fifty, it says to me. The chances of surviving the consecutive missteps I've made on that day reveal themselves in stone: fifty-fifty.

The previous night around the campfire, I lamented my regret to Tim, an Iraq Special Operations Forces veteran and neighboring camper at Big Lagoon County Park, of not combing Trinidad's beaches for precious agates while I instead walked parallel on a car-choked avenue just a quarter-mile east. Tim suggested I adjust my route to walk along the shore connecting one beach car lot to another, making miles on sand rather than pavement.

It plays deeply to my sensibilities, so without much inquiry, I acquiesce to his suggestion and adjust my plans. A morning stroll on the beach it is. Unfortunately, my unchecked enthusiasm overcomes my usual cautious attention to detail, thereby causing me to abandon an important logistical consideration: the day's tidal chart.

As the moon's influence pulls waves inward and up, I too succumb to its force as it pushes me against the cliffs as water rises. Must I also rise? I make my second poor decision of the morning as I think, *If I can just get up these 250-foot cliffs, I can rock climb my way to safety.* It is as if my practical self washed out to sea, leaving me with the intelligence of driftwood (apologies to driftwood).

I grab a small rock outcrop to inch my unskilled sixty-year-old body slowly towards the precipice of the slippery cliff as the weight of my fully-loaded backpack taunts me, tugging my attention towards the craggy beach below. If I survive—it's not the first time I've bandied these words about—I promise never to go off route again.

It's not the first time I make a promise I won't keep. Though I'm shaken, weak, and muddy, each foot placement inexplicably works in my favor. Good rock climbers climb with their eyes, I am told. I climb with my gut.

At last, I top the cliff only to realize that elevation heightens my troubles with bramble to my right, bramble to my left, and bramble, dense wood, and more bramble between me and US 101. As I cautiously make my way north, thorns tattoo my exposed arms and legs with bloody hash marks. Planting my walking stick on top of the bushes, I flatten down branches and, to minimize lacerations, balance on the stick like a tightrope walker. And thus I slowly tiptoe a trail forward as the tide below licks its lips at me.

Bad decision number three.

And so, I plod on. I have no game plan. I only know the beach far below to my left has disappeared under salty water while a quick assessment to my right suggests the futility of any attempt to reach the road. No one knows where I am except Special Forces Tim, who has no reason to give any thought to my welfare, though he would be someone to bank on in such a predicament.

As I consider my options, something again catches me off guard. A deep, wide, rocky, and muddy ravine stops me in my tracks. Or lack thereof, for the pliable bramble pops right up behind me to catch my backpack with every step, leaving no trace of me in my wake.

Damn! This is what happens when I don't follow my spreadsheet.

I wait . . . but I'm not sure what for. I perceive no way around the ravine. The day grows cold and cloudy, and so does my mind.

I make more promises I won't keep, because this won't be my last act of stupidity. But, by God, it won't be my last act, I convince myself! And with that declaration, I shock myself out of idleness. This is my Hail Mary moment, I sigh as I clasp my belongings to my chest. I take a gamble out of desperation, get on my butt, and slide down the ravine creating a thirty-six-yard avalanche of mud, rock, and me.

I've traveled less than six miles all day. I'm soaked head to foot in mud. I bleed from every exposed limb and itch between the scrapes from what I will soon identify as poison sumac. I haven't eaten all day and have four hours between me and the nearest meal. But in an instant, bowing in gratitude to solid ground that's supported me for nearly 5,500 miles thus far, I pluck a small stone from the sand and am suddenly, fully, and radiantly joyful.

I prostrate to Jesus and to Buddha, and hail praises to Mary and Archangel Michael and every celestial being who has my back. I am alive! Death had its chance with me, but I and my cosmic support team score a miracle touchdown.

Enough is enough, I scold myself. Time to stop lugging my egocentric pain around in my backpack—my pity pack, as it were. It's a heavy load to carry, and I can't afford its weight. I don't want to end up alive despite the odds predicted in stone only to endure life the way Brenda sees her customers—as never fully living while waiting to die. I want more. I owe myself more. I'm not afraid of death, I just don't want it to visit me just then.

I continue north until I come upon Philip half sitting on the picnic table taking a cigarette break as I call to him to inquire about food. "Cross the bridge, and you'll find a restaurant on the left. Tell my partner Johnathan to make you something with love." That's just what I need, just what I order, and just what I'm served—fourteen miles up the road from the awakening of my slumber at the world famous Palm Café in Orick, three days south of Oregon, and seven thousand miles east of hell.

If Patna is hell, then an overnight in Orick is practice for purgatory. After my heavenly gravy-smothered chicken fried steak with gravy-smothered mashed potato mountains, a family-sized serving of grilled veggies, and biscuits dripping in butter (honestly, I do not have a death wish!), I covertly plant my tent on the lawn of the South Operations Center of Redwood National Park.

I'm careful to shield myself from headlights of employees driving in and out of the gated compound as well as from parking-lot floodlights of the Orick Market across the street. A metal fence stands between me and the restaurant's dumpsters where much of the night's activity takes place except for the critters that find equal enjoyment exploring my tent. All night long, they bump me, sniff me, and squeak their squeaky voices at me. I don't get much sleep.

I rise at six-thirty on Easter morning. I dust dried mud from my walking clothes, sluggishly brush my teeth behind the compound's landscaped trees, and carelessly stuff my gear into my bag before I shuffle past the dumpster hotel to the Palm Café for a thick slice of banana cream pie and several cups of hot, better-than-adequate black coffee. I take my first delicious bite and am instantly transported to my Grandma Kender's apartment in Worcester, Massachusetts—which is to say the pie crust must have been made with gobs of memory-invoking lard. Familiar, nostalgic, and containing enough calories and fruit for one day's walking. All is well.

Not until months later do I learn the world famous café is permanently shuttered for multiple health violations. I jocosely wonder where all my varmint sleepmates will get their next meals.

Though my toes ache from the pressure of the fiasco of the previous day, I am able to walk timidly in awe through Redwoods National Forest along the Newton B. Drury Scenic Parkway. The air is heavy with dew, and endless shades of green sparkle in incessant streams of sunlight that pierce the treetops. I salute the ancient 1,500-year-old, 286-foot Big Tree and meditate at the base of the Spiral Redwood. My pace grinds to a halt as I admire their stature. Unable to see their crowns from my miniature perspective, I crank my neck as far back as I can before my pack threatens to topple me.

I don't know why, but there's only so much beauty I can endure before I have to look away. If, for example, a majestic green swallowtail were to alight on my nose, because of our intimacy, I could not take it all in. I would close my eyes for not wanting it to flit away. I likewise breathe in the forest as much as my being can absorb and hold in its grandeur behind closed eyelids. A soft urging, like the wings of a butterfly, spurs me to once again open my eyes only to discover the forest shimmering in a kaleidoscope of emerald, and I once again succumb to the allure of the giants.

The road is mine to own with a scant few travelers at this time of year. Early spring tourists mostly meander in their cars just as I do on foot, but one must be prepared for the locals who use an isolated strip of pavement as their own personal speedway. The phenomenon holds true for many beautiful backroads around the country.

Rural America is generally a forgotten America, or so I hear as I foray into isolated pockets, such as in the Redwoods, through the states. Forgotten America also tends to harbor places where God, family, and country matter most—in that order. Of all the responses received to my inquiry "What matters most in life?," spirituality ranks high, and God and Jesus factor in greatly along with other master-full expressions of spiritual life such as a Higher Power, Mother-Father God, Divine Source, All That Is, Unity Consciousness, or, as Andy whom I met in Florida said, the eyeballs and tongue of God.

It isn't until I'm in Florida when a woman answers with the familiar trinity "God, family, country" followed by a sincere question, "Are you packing?" that I know I must dig deeper. I really need to get my head around how God, as I understand God, co-exists within a cultural obsession with firearms. So, I attempt to unpack the practice of packing.

I fire my first pistol in Georgia. I do not carry a gun despite the urging of a few family members. Chris and my brother-in-law Al own a sporting goods store, and they'd be glad to fit me with just the right handgun for my safety if I am so inclined.

I am not.

"There's more than one way," I remind myself.

As I walk south along Route 17 in Spring Bluff in early 2015, coping with eighty-eight degrees of unprotected sunshine, I stop at a yard sale with Christie Binzen, my walking partner through Jacksonville. We recognize the woman presiding over the sale as our server from the night before at Zackry's Seafood Restaurant. Just as we welcome both the shade and iced drinks Trish offers, we hear shots from behind the house. During a break in his target practice, Trish introduces us to her husband Tim. He's been giving his wife shooting lessons and nonchalantly offers to give me one, too.

I automatically—and somewhat astonishingly—accept.

My legs slightly bent, my back straight and shoulders down, I hold Tim's Berretta as he taught me. I hold the grip of the gun with my right hand, resting my trigger finger along the side of the barrel. I cup the butt of the grip underneath with my left hand for support. Careful not to lock my elbows, I then extend my arms so as to look straight down the barrel. There's a lot to think about to get this right.

The paper target is a black silhouette of a person's upper torso. The gun is heavy and too big for me, but after some hesitation, I pull hard with my index finger to simultaneously cock and release the hammer.

Ka-pow!

To my great shock, I hit the target in the throat. As a peace-loving person, I amuse myself at how elated I am with my success. It feels contrary to who I am. I know, of course, that individuals are complex and can hold seemingly opposing views. But I point to that moment when I begin to release tendencies to place limiting definitions upon myself. Rockets of change that awareness eventually triggers will continue to surprise me for years to come.

I still don't pack a gun. When asked if I am carrying, which happens in every state I pass through, I answer with a wink and a smile, "I'm protected." That seems to pacify a person's concern. I do not correct their assumptions. No one has to know that the protection I speak of comes from a far less tangible source.

While I can't contort my terrestrial body back far enough to see the capstones of impressive Redwoods, I know the treetops are there. Though my view doesn't take it all in, I know the forest exists. My vantage point from the ground is enough for now. Likewise, I cannot deny the presence of an Infinite Creator. I can only point towards Divinity through my direct experience of its handiwork. I am not carrying; I am being carried. I walk protected—without the added weight to my pack or staring down the barrel of my values.

Now when people tell me they put Jesus, Allah, Jehovah, or Yahweh first, I am curious how they put their feet to their faith. In a nutshell, the answers are the same. Live by the Golden Rule. In everything you do, do to others what you would have them do to you. Simply put, be kind—or in other words, live like the Bluebirds' Cecile.

At my panoramic review after my Dad greets me from his golf cart, and I get a big bear hug from Al (yes, brother-in-law Al) and dance through the tunnel of light with my Mom, I hope to hear, "Paula mostly served others over self, and she was mostly kind."

Those are the big guns I carry. That's what I'm packing.

September 21, 2019
International Day of Peace
41.4220°N, 82.3646°W
Vermilion, Ohio

A Happiness Walker and a Flower Lady walk into town, begins the story. It sounds like the start of a joke, but it's far from that. It's how my host Dana Corogin, who colors her town with prisms of summer petals, introduces me to a Vietnam ex-prisoner of war, Harlan Chapman, who lives on the shore of Lake Erie. Harlan, a lieutenant colonel in the US Marine Corps, was shot down over a rice paddy near Hai Duong on November 5, 1965, and subsequently tortured and imprisoned at the infamous Hanoi Hilton for seven years and three months. In his understated manner, he describes the treatment he received as cruel.

"A door handle."

"Excuse me?" I ask.

"A handle on the inside of a door . . . freedom. That's what matters," he softly and poignantly answers my question. Unable to coherently respond or do justice to the gravity of his reply, I bite my lip and freeze.

I recover enough to hear more. Harlan relied heavily on his minimal contacts with others by tapping in code through thick concrete walls. "In unity is strength," he continues. "They understood that and tried to keep us separated." The captors attempted to break the spirit of one by detaching him from the many. What they didn't understand is they could never separate a man from the One.

Harlan prayed a lot and kept faith that the code of honor never to leave a man behind would be upheld for himself and for the other prisoners. He told of a young sailor who ended up in prison "by accident." Before his release and with the help of his comrades, he memorized all the names of the more than three hundred prisoners of war through song to inform anxious and hopeful families back home of their status.

"You have to be an optimist," Harlan said. "What other choice do you have?"

Happiness or sadness is in your brain—your head," continues Harlan. "I feel sad for the people who don't see their choices."

He finishes with the wisdom of someone who understands the importance of his words. "Just be a nice person." Like so many others, even after the unspeakable cruelties of his life, Harlan believes in the power of the Golden Rule.

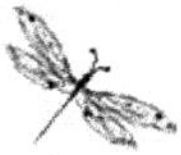

photo by Paula Francis

Toaster House proprietor Nita Larrone displays a photo from the 1940 Pie Town Festival in front of a later photo of the same women, including her mother. Out of view: Nina's stuffed and mounted pelican perched on a banister on October 5, 2016, at 3,726 miles during Leg 10 of the Happiness Walk.

BASIC HAPPY SHIT

"What can each of us do to make this a better world?" I ask.
"Be like a Golden Retriever," he responds.

—Anonymous
Beaufort, South Carolina

October 5, 2016
34.2984°N, 108.1348°W
Pie Town, New Mexico

"Don't worry," says Nita Larronde as she pours two golden shots of Damiana, a soothing Mexican concoction with ancient Mayan roots. "He barely smells." Nita smirks as she points to the mounted pelican on the second-floor railing of her house overlooking her extensive collection of international knickknacks.

My fellow travelers and I have already received a tour of her town, including a visit to the very first antenna of the Very Long Baseline Array, VLBA. While privileged to see that hidden gem, I recently strutted past twenty-seven such telescopes just two days east. You may recognize them from their portrayal in the movie *Contact* where Jodie Foster's character finds an encoded message from the Vega star system. At the moment, and may I say quite unlike me, I am more curious about the pelican in her living room than the giant galactic eyeglasses.

199

Nita is proprietor of the Toaster House in Pie Town, New Mexico, where she proudly raised her five children before moving to her newer, pelican-festooned home. She kept the Toaster House as a hostel just two miles west of the Continental Divide for through hikers and cyclists, most of whom travel the nearby Pacific Crest Trail. Rustic and well-stocked, it is decorated with toasters on the inside and out, on arbors, in trees, and on every inch of fence. A rainbow of worn, mud-caked sneakers—discarded for a new version of themselves by travelers who left them behind—adorn the porch wall.

Its own concierge of sorts anticipates the needs of those who patronize the hostel. Ajo's white beard reaches below his chest. He sports a ball cap, a well-worn sweatshirt, and a skirt. I am told his attire is formal, given his preference for no clothes at all.

Generous, observant of detail, and equipped with a library of stories, Ajo listens attentively to yours. Since the closest grocery store is eighty-three miles east in Socorro, it isn't without active listening and careful planning that a bag labeled Happiness Walker appears in the porch fridge with my favorite beer and nutritious traveling snacks.

Ajo ascribes to the philosophy of Jonathan Blodgett, the cook who made me a plate of chicken fried love on Easter eve who said, "I think happiness is to be one human race, to be holding hands with your brother. You see somebody on the street and they're hungry, feed them. Simple things like that, basic happy shit." That's what Ajo dishes out. He sees every Toaster House adventurer as a brother or sister and blesses them with basic happy shit.

Once upon a time, there was no pie in Pie Town. Clyde Norman, an enterprising baker, established the first pie shop in 1920 for those traveling westward towards better futures.

According to locals, bakeries flourished. And then they didn't. Route 40 to the north and Route 10 to the south made the middle Route 60 through Pie Town obsolete and the pies superfluous.

Luckily for me, Chocolate, Coconut and Banana Cream with Meringue, Apple, Apple Cranberry Crumb, Cheer-y Cherry, Starry Starry Blueberry Night, Very Berry, Peachy Keen, Chocolate Chess with Red Chile, New Mexico Apple with Pine Nuts, and Peach Green Chile pies all made a comeback in time for my empty belly. I eat pie for breakfast and again for dinner several days in a row. I am ahead of schedule, so I can afford to stay in one place and gorge myself on sweet, sour, and savory concoctions.

With a whopping population of ninety-three residents, Pie Town has more than one claim to fame. It is also a recognized Dark Skies Defender, a designation not casually given to locations around the globe that effectively guard against light pollution. Tucked with an expanded stomach in my sleeping bag on the top bunk in Toaster House's annex, I glimpse a sliver of stars also captured by the VLBA telescopes. The night sky is as clear and bejeweled as I've ever witnessed. I feel insignificant yet simultaneously connected to all that exists. I am consumed by the vast emptiness among galaxies, stars, planets, and atoms. I am satiated by the beauty, sugar-coated stars, and all-out brilliance of the cosmos.

But as my new friend Dr. Clinton Bliss of Seattle cautions, "My favorite thing is the combination of truth and beauty—and truth is often ugly."

Four days later and several pie pounds heavier, I carry the weight of that understanding when, at last, I continue on to California through lands once home to Navajo or Dine', Hopi,

Mohave, Gila, Akimel O'odham or Pima, Maricopa or Pee-Posh, and Apache peoples and so violently stolen from them in the name of American progress.

I plead ignorance when it comes to the true history of the "founding" of my country. My schoolbooks did not recount the disturbing history of slave trade that tore people from their ancestral roots nor of settler colonialism including deceit and trauma bestowed upon indigenous peoples who inhabited this land for twelve thousand or more years before colonists arrived. My school texts surely did not honor sophisticated and thriving pre-colonial communities that influenced the US Constitution of today.

So when people say that what they wish for most is to go back in time to a simpler life—and they often do say that, I wonder which era they refer to and which versions of history are stamped into their consciousness.

I know I am guilty, too. I romanticize the times when, as a child, I roamed free the entire day in my neighborhood only to return home after my mother rang the cow bell for a six o'clock dinner. I covet the times when my young children sat around the dinner table talking about their school days or playing board games that lasted for hours or singing around the campfire as we toasted marshmallows without electronics to distract us.

And as I write these words, how I long for the days before pandemics, quarantines, wildfires, and insurrections—and the days when I gorged on pie and marveled at the vast and arresting sky.

Yet, as valid as such longings seem, they negate the foundation of advantaged positions, the foundation that fortified and continues to fortify our nation based on inequities, injustices, domination, deception, greed, and endless war.

Dr. Bliss had it right. There is an ugly truth swept under our American rug. And the whole truth needs illumination so we can step with honesty and transparency into the future nourished by the beauty of creation.

History paves the roads we walk. Our choices beget the repetition of our past or can give rise to a new era steeped in the Golden Rule. It's up to us to pull on the door handle of freedom and walk into truth, as unfamiliar as the path may be.

Forging a new future is unlikely to occur along a straight line. My day-by-day journey more resembles a spiral. With the goal of making distance, I find myself advancing towards familiar horizons as my orientation constantly changes. Distances blur as I circle past intended milestones. A déjà vu of multiple events swirls through my memory, yet everything on every day is new.

By 2016, I can predict the ebb and flow of nomadic life. Still, I sense no forewarning of the hairpin turn awaiting me in Hawaii.

First, though, I must cross the formidable Mojave Desert.

October 5, 2016
34.1500°N, 114.2891°W
Parker, Arizona

More than a hundred miles stretch between me and Twentynine Palms, California, and another eighteen miles to the campground where I hope to stay. I factor in three hours of travel to and from my starting points plus time to secure safe places with food and water at night. I calculate the diminishing hours of daylight and conclude I have six twenty-plus mile days of desert walking to Joshua Tree. I have no idea how I will manage, only a certainty that I will.

I make it in five.

Long before Spanish explorers, Desert Indians used the low lying corridor between mountains to establish trade routes between tribes. Remnants of early trails resemble the Nazca

Lines in Peru, as viewed from above. Other trails vanish under pavement. Guided by ancient footprints and historic wagon wheel ruts below my feet, I walk the present-day road in the way of Kokopelli, traveling singularly and calling in the changing of seasons with my feathers and a flowering mind.

The company of history feels palpable.

For a couple of days, I make my home base in Parker, Arizona, as I negotiate my way along CA-62 W, otherwise known as Twentynine Palms Highway.

This is going to take a lot of coffee.

I've left Dead Man's trailer all cleaned up, including the grotesque, moldy encrusted bathroom, and have checked in to the Kafa Inn. I stay for two days and get a ride back and forth to my starting and ending points. In a convenience store at the junction where Parker Dam veers off to the right and I to the left, a woman offers me a magic marker and piece of cardboard. She politely informs me that thumbing a ride is unlawful in California—whose state line I have just crossed. Oddly, hitching a ride with a sign is not.

It works. A motorhome stops almost immediately. Phil Murphy transports me to my start, but I know I can't keep the back and forth up forever. Distances and isolation exceed anything I've experienced since Texas, yet I don't see any other way to proceed. Phil seems a bit confused but accommodating and oddly disappointed to let me out when he reaches Vidal Junction. The only human in sight is a Border Protection Station inspector concerned with illegal interstate produce. Unless you count pilfered hotel jelly packets, I have none.

Often not seeing vehicles for several minutes in either direction, I walk the vast desert. My view is straight and long. Mirages appear through waves as heat rises from the dusty brown, barren landscape. Though too hot for wildlife, it is just right for me.

I want to paint it. I haven't painted in years, but shades of brown, shadows of the mountains, and the silence of the space stir me. Occasional delicate, white blossoms manifest ever more beautiful for their will to push through gravel and rise towards the sun.

There is no shade. Spiny shrubs lie low. Sand. Rock. Sky. Infinity.

I belong here.

A passing motorcyclist screeches to a skidding stop. Unfortunately, as he does, he blows out his front tire. I wait with him while he calls for help and discover he is on a road trip from Massachusetts, close to where I once lived. We make plans for his friend to bring me back to Parker after repairs to his bike. His bad fortune is my kismet.

But I have a plan B and C for a reason. His friends don't show for me. I hope they showed for him. It's late, and I decide I could, if I have to, camp in the desert. I change the sign I've been flashing at scant passersby from RIDE, PLEASE to WATER, PLEASE! I've been rationing my water all day, and I'll need more if I'm staying the night out here.

I came to know Dylan Cuddy through my nonagenarian, running-across-the-country friend, Mr. Ernie. We inhabit the same long-distance tribe, but my walk across the south qualifies as a crawl compared to Dylan's straight-through cross-country trek.

We both hail from and began our trips from New England. He starts long after me and ends long before me, so I benefit from his experiences. I remember some of his advice and how he once fashioned a hammock to camp beneath railroad tracks that parallel the very road I travel. I don't have the same gear, but I talk myself into believing I can rig something up to get off the ground so snakes don't sleep with me.

"There is no rattler season in the desert," he warned me.

People do provide water—by throwing bottles out their windows as they slow down a tad before they speed away. I must look pretty scary. At least I end up with enough water to hydrate overnight. Another biker, Julian, kindly stops but apologetically can't give me a ride for lack of an extra helmet. Instead, he hands me his last cold, throat-quenching, energy drink along with the lone sandwich in his pack. I return half the sandwich, and we eat together, standing on the side of the highway: sun setting, temperatures cooling, and traffic waning.

I feel settled with my plans for the evening.

As I move west looking for a place to set up camp, along comes Tim. Tim Hutcherson opens his cooler full of iced water and offers me as many as I can consume on the spot and more to tuck in my pack. He explains he doesn't want to interrupt my progress. Otherwise, he would offer me a ride to Joshua Tree, where he is passing through.

I pause. I collect words that blink like fireflies within my mind to carefully fashion my response, then gingerly clarify how I would very much appreciate a ride and how it wouldn't be an imposition nor at all interrupt my walk.

I haven't met many people who so keenly grasp my need to connect each mile. Many times a day, I waive off offers of rides. But now does not demand such facility. I wholeheartedly choose and gratefully accept eighty miles per hour by car over three miles per hour by foot and the safety of a campground over an adventure under train trestles.

I am not Dylanesque. He, by the way, transitioned into a peace walk in Rwanda and most recently put his talents to work as a medic in the US Army.

Dylan inspires me in so many ways!

As for me, I'm just trying to sketch out a plan for how to retrace the remaining miles on foot that Tim now transports me by truck. It's helpful to see the terrain I will walk before I actually walk it, even through darkness. I spontaneously decide to take the next day off, and my body relaxes in the cushion of time I've just created to figure things out later. For now, I'm thrilled not to share my tent in the wilderness, days from civilization, with four-season snakes.

After we grab dinner, Tim drops me off at the Joshua Tree Retreat Center where primitive camping is allowed. We agree to stay in touch, and some days later, he and his lovely extended family host me in their town one walking day east of Los Angeles. From there, finding hosts for the next several legs up the Pacific Coast will be—well, easy as pie!

As I make my way through the Sheephole Valley Wilderness and Joshua Tree National Park sections of the Mojave, I follow aqueducts just to my north. The 242-mile-long channel diverts a billion gallons of daily water flow from the Colorado River to urban southern California. I am not surprised to observe protective forces overseeing the intricate tunnels and pumping stations. The early sinking sun glistens on metal pipes and bounces reflective rays off military instillations otherwise camouflaged at the base of the hills.

Water. The issue is always water in the desert. It equates to Sahara gold.

My body has acclimated like a camel's—traveling long stretches with minimal depletion of supplies. I balance fluid intake and output with great precision and am careful not to dehydrate while also minimizing the need to stop. After much practice, I have learned to pee on the side of the road in ten seconds flat between passing cars and without taking off my large backpack. It's an annoyance, but the alternative of not needing to urinate is much worse.

Oh, what I'd give for the toilets of India.

On an early November day, I reach a total of 4,200 miles ambled since I began the Happiness Walk. I left my backpack at camp, so I've stuffed all my needs into a hip pack. Two fluffernutter sandwiches melt to mush there in their respective breakfast and lunch plastic bags. The messy sandwiches will provide me necessary sustenance for walking the remainder of the 2016 presidential election week across a truly awe inspiring American landscape.

A good time to be alone, I reflect.

Dylan comes through again. Through social media, he introduces me to Shannan Limon, my newest and most generous road angel. Shannan hosted Dylan as he passed through Twentynine Palms months before. "What do you need?" she asks as I answer her call.

"Oh, my. My needs are many. Do you really want to know?"

For three mornings, Shannan picks me up from the campground before sunrise and indulges me with a large, hot, black Starbucks coffee. We drive the ninety, sixty, or thirty miles to my start and drop gallons of water at strategic stations along the way. As the winter sun begins to wane behind the mountains, she picks me up with a basket of hot food for my dinner. She pampers me like that throughout the Mojave.

Why does she do such a thing in the midst of a busy life and active family schedule? "I want to teach my kids altruism," she replies.

Kindness is a simple thing to offer. We've all heard stories of how an act of kindness can make the difference between life and death. While not quite that, Shannan surely makes a difference for me between hardship and joy. As with Nita and Ajo, her kindness is the bedrock of her existence. I'd say that's a great lesson to teach any child.

"I don't have to know you to help you," echoes Dr. Mekah Gordon, a Santa Fe professor of goldsmithing and silversmithing who quips that she also works in kryptonite. In a similar vein, my road angels are also alchemists who magically transmute uncertainties of the road into experiences I will cherish forever. They may not use kryptonite or wear capes, but if they did, they would be emblazoned with BHSH: Basic Happy Shit Hero. I naturally have faith in humanity, but my faith resides evermore fierce because of all the heroes and heroines of kindness I've encountered—who use their powers to make someone else's life a little bit better.

Dr. Mekah might also say, "I don't have to know you to see you have cape-worthy qualities." Life can be tough. Labyrinths can be complicated. You may have stinky pelicans in your home or scary rattlers under your trestles. We share a history difficult to face, and life's outward appearance may look increasingly grim. Though fallible, imperfect, and a tiny crystalline speck of the cosmos, we can all be alchemists of our circumstance.

When I look to the stars and contemplate the vastness of the universe, I can easily believe in a purpose for the unveiling chaos and ionospheric changes on our planet and in our lives. Everything else seems so elegantly ordered: the cycles of time, the progression of the equinox, the evolution of humanity. We each have to make sense of our experiences in our own way, but I believe each member of our collective faces their own hero's journey. Our shadows shout, "This is what you don't want. Discard your spreadsheet. Make a U-turn. Warm your face in the sun, and walk in the light."

I don't want to go back to a simpler time, because there is no such thing. I want—in the present lifetime—what Dr Bliss wants: truth and beauty . . . and a slice of happiness pie.

To quote my wig-wearing, karaoke-singing new friend Kristie from Utah, "There is no triumph without trial." There have been challenges behind me, and I know there will be challenges before me. But I never expect the utopia of Hawaii to cough up so many bold, nauseating, and gut-wrenching blows.

Unprotected by distant shores, I see my lessons keep on coming. At least on the islands, they are served up with fresh pineapple.

Paula places ashes of her brother-in-law Al Noyes into the Snake River in Wendell, Idaho, after her camp hosts drove her to a place Al would have loved for a private ceremony on October 28, 2016 at 6,746 miles during Leg 15 of the Happiness Walk.

A BOMB AND A BOMBSHELL

When we meet death, we are able to see all the connecting links. The song has been sung and you sang it well and you feel gratified and you are ready to embrace death.

—Elizabeth Chapman
Holyoke, Massachusetts

"You have arrived," the GPS lady tells me. And I believe I have. It looks like the paradise of my dreams.

Gina Overton, my friend from thirty-five years before, greets me with an orange and green lei strung with shells and nuts. I wear it proudly. Somehow, she hasn't aged at all. We slide right into the friendship we once enjoyed in our post-college, pre-marriage days. She is like that—easy, interested, and interesting.

Gina takes me to her house to get acclimated. I intend to circumambulate O'ahu and four other Hawaiian islands before I take a short vacation with my west-coast daughter in utopia, otherwise known as Kauai.

January 16, 2018
21.3069°N, 157.8583°W
Honolulu, Hawaii

I was still residing in my father's house after his death when I returned to the road. I resumed in LA, walked six hundred miles to San Francisco to spend Thanksgiving with my daughter, flew back east to spend Christmas with the rest of my family, then flew nineteen hours back across the continent and half of the Pacific Ocean to Hawaii.

After a mere eight days, I am already exhausted and wholly unprepared for the remainder of the trip. On half of the eight days, I write in my journal, "Something is off. I'm off." Like a foreboding message stuffed in a fortune cookie, I should have taken heed when a so-called bomb cyclone dumped snow on Boston and my flight was delayed by twenty-four hours.

I slowly circumambulate the lush, tropical island counter-clockwise from Honolulu three quarters around to Waianae. Exiting the community center where I've interviewed several locals picking up their food bank packages in this land of abundance, I receive the call. I ingest it in shattered pieces.

It's my Vermont neighbor, Dawn McCall.

Tragedy strikes the neighborhood.

A young man, a good soul who lost his way, has been shot dead.

I can't walk. My legs don't move. I collapse at the gate.

I grieve over his confused life. I grieve for his loving parents.

I stay pinned to the ground until a bus stops nearby. I go where it goes. It doesn't matter.

I am so exhausted.

Three days earlier, I set out on another sun-filled, cloudless sapphire sky morning to enjoy the picturesque shoreline of Kailua Beach. I have just finished interviewing Orlando, a boxer one match away from a world championship who sports a cauliflower ear as proof.

My phone buzzes. As I retrieve the message, my eyes catch the stillness around me—everyone commanded to their phones. It's 8:07 AM on Tuesday.

BALLISTIC MISSILE THREAT INBOUND TO HAWAII.
SEEK SHELTER. THIS IS NOT A DRILL.

My thoughts kick into overdrive: *There's no sense finding shelter because a bomb will destroy everything. A bomb will undoubtedly target the harbors of O'ahu. We'll be incinerated. It's over. Call my girls, tell them how much I love them. Don't tell them about the missile. They will find out. Focus on love. I am okay with dying. It's funny that I'm dying in paradise.*

Who's that guy? He hasn't heard. He should know in case he wants to do something—say something. Am I dying with this stranger? Ask his name.

Thirty-eight minutes. That's how much time elapses before the message is retracted.

Time is an illusion. You can't measure thirty-eight minutes of waiting for imminent death.

It will take weeks before the true story of events gets out—if it ever does.

I met José, the hired assassin, four days earlier. I wonder what his Archangel Michael has to say today. "I fought for you, you are safe now," seems about right!

The common experience creates a bond among us on the island, although I feel I've already begun to find my hanai or adopted family. Kimo and I meet over Spam and eggs at the KOA, not the campground, but a pancake house in the residential community of Hawaii Kai.

Kimo is either much older than I or hasn't aged very well. He hails from a family of drinkers, but for all that, he does not. His stubble is specked with gray as is his curly, shoulder-length, dark hair, which matches the dark tone of his weathered skin. Bushy eyebrows sit below the rim of his red baseball cap. He sports three long fingernails on his right hand as natural picks for his guitar, and when he laughs, he giggles like a child.

"He-he," he spits out as he shyly covers his mouth.

Kimo isn't partial to photographs nor voice recordings, so I draw his picture in my journal to capture his image. He does, nevertheless, share a great deal of wisdom and history as he tours me around his island in his beat-up car. We meet up five separate times during my short stay, and we will meet again when he hosts me upon my return to the island. But it won't happen the way we plan.

Trust, caring for others as he did for his wife for ten years through Alzheimer's, truth, responsibility, and most of all—righteousness. Those are some things that matter to Kimo.

My new friend narrowly escaped death twice, he tells me. Once, after a truck collided with his youthful body, he was not expected to live when a stranger came to his hospital room and prayed him back to health. Ultimately, he sustained only a slight limp that he sports today. Later as a teen, while spear fishing off Waimanalo Beach, he barely evaded a shark. He distracted the carnivorous fish by expertly tossing bait away from him as he appealed to his savior. Once again, he survived through prayer. Kimo would not call the experiences miraculous. He would call them the hand of God.

By evading a missile, he eludes death a third time.

"The end of the world is coming," Kimo suggests. "Have no fear. It's God's will.

"You, however," he tells me, "will live over one hundred years—mark my words."

Kimo didn't flinch during the missile mishap. And he didn't flinch when the end of the week brought what my southern friends would call toad-strangling rain, the likes of which haven't been seen for ten years when there were forty days and forty nights of deluge on O'ahu.

Biblical.

Such is nirvana.

Bullfrogs sing their love songs as fog envelops the striking emerald Ko'olau mountain range. The sun brushes rainbows on water droplets clinging to gigantic palm leaves. Ukulele music pervades the shops with roosters as backup vocalists. We receive a call, we get a text, and like the surfers, we all just ride the waves.

I walk through Kimo's childhood neighborhood of Waimanalo, a homesteading community that serves native Hawaiians but only if a government agent determines someone worthy to claim the heritage.

I walk the plastic-strewn beaches of Kahana Bay collecting non-biodegradable trash from long distance shores and sea dumps.

I stroll through Chinatown and past Waikiki's posh infinity pools and cabanas.

I walk industrial areas, neglected and impoverished districts, and homeless camps where it is unlawful to sit or lie down.

I sip umbrellaed Mai Tais with fresh pineapple garnishes at Turtle Bay, watch a fire dance at sunset, and kayak in Kaneohe Bay.

I swim at Halona Blowhole Cove, a location featured in several movies including the classic *From Here to Eternity.*

I eat spam and hot dogs and Subway sandwiches.

I watch humpback whales, step around beached harbor seals, marvel at colorful parrots, and walk with dragonflies.

I am so, so tired.

Two Facebook posts reveal the shocking divorce of a friend

and a third suicide within my close knit Vermont community after two recent blows that also shook us to our core. All that, even as we mourn the still fresh news about the shooting death of my Vermont neighbor.

I had been told to be alert to ionospheric changes that will wreak havoc on the planet. I had no idea they would hit so close to home.

I, too, post to Facebook. That's how I communicate about the project to the public and how I stay connected to new and old friends. I dislike the chore of posting, but it furthers the cause of the GNHUSA mission. So, when I receive sincere feedback from a follower that I shouldn't send updates from sunny Hawaii as New England experiences a dismaying cold snap, I snap. I can't help it, I do—luckily, not at the person or online, but silently.

The realization smacks me that we each hold our own point of view based on where we stand. I learn the metaphorical lesson taught and retaught every day as I roam the land if not every day in life. The lesson becomes more essential for me going forward as I realize I must have a 360° point of view while listening to each individual with whom I speak.

I must acknowledge the ionospheric conditions permeating each life.

I try to see the view of the Facebook commenter, which is the best I can do. Hailing from New England, I imagine that individual's orientation involves high snowbanks, frosted windows, and a great yearning for an umbrellaed tropical drink while sitting in a beach chair.

I must, too, be ever so vigilant and know my place.

I put down my phone and advance to the nearest food truck for a malasada—a yummy Hawaiian doughnut—to sooth myself.

I will surely need to break the doughnut-eating habit post walk.

So that was dramatic reads the text from one of my daughters, referring neither to the missile nor the deaths nor the divorce nor the snowstorm.

Oh, boy, yet another drama on the horizon. It is only then that I tell her about the events of the week. I am already aching for my daughter and me to be in Kauai before I even leave the first of the islands. The drama she speaks of turns out to be regular people drama. Oh, how I wish we would learn there's enough of that to go around without conjuring up new stuff.

My GPS lady helps navigate me to my hosts' home in Kaneohe. I am connected to Sharon and Barry Usagawa through a Vermont friend, Jack Pransky, who helped me repair the hole in my heart. I am further introduced to others through his network of colleagues. That leads me to hosts Rita and Cam Shuford in Kailua and another dramatic turn. Shockingly, shortly after my stay, Cam, a vibrant and athletic man will succumb to a heart attack while bicycling. After all the heinous events of the week, I should not be surprised.

But the spiral keeps on twisting, turning, and moving me inward and outward while blinding me at hairpin turns. One wild, abrupt detour catapults me 4,900 miles to North Carolina.

It is four o'clock in the morning Hawaiian time when my phone rings. "Well, this isn't good," I think to myself, then say out loud to my sister when I answer.

"It's not," Chris whispers through tears. "Al's dead."

My big ole, bear-hugging, belly-laughing, bald-headed, big-hearted brother-in-law is dead.

I am numb, but I can't afford to collapse. Collapsing is a luxury. I get the basic information before she needs to attend to her immediate needs.

Al died on the plane. Chris is in Greenville, North Carolina? But they were headed to Las Vegas. This was supposed to be a vacation. Al's dead. How could he be dead? He's only sixty. What happened? How can this happen? Oh, my God—Chris! She's all alone. I need to get a flight out now. Pack my bags. Leave a note for Sharon and Barry. Call a taxi.

CHRISSSSSSSSSY!

I gather my things as quietly as possible and bring my bag downstairs. Barry enters the kitchen as I write a note. He doesn't take no for an answer and insists on driving me across the island to the airport. The women at the ticket counter make several calls in hushed tones to arrange the earliest direct flight at a significantly reduced rate. They bring me to their lounge for priority passengers so I can make some private calls and rest until I catch the flight from paradise to yet another hell, this one the worst.

A bomb cyclone marked the beginning of this leg, a bomb threat rained down in the middle, and a bombshell dropped in the end. I need to take such signs more seriously.

Kimo blesses the water every day. He goes to the beach and acknowledges its life-giving nature. Unlike me, he understands and respects the power of water without requiring the scientific proof I seemed to need. When I later walk in Idaho, a place Al loved for its raw, abundant beauty and wilderness, I scatter some of his ashes into the rushing, crystalline water of the Snake River and bless its life-giving and life-transmuting nature and respect the power of an in-breath.

I return to Hawaii a month and a half later. My daughter Julia joins me in Kauai, where we get our much needed vacation. As we make our way to the Kauai Coffee Company and planta-tion, a white owl crosses directly in our path—twice. The birds, known in Hawaii as pueo, are steeped in local folklore and, I'm told, rarely seen. They are considered aumakua or ancestral guardians that protect the family from harm.

Not about to miss yet another sign, I take this one to heart. As my jaunt continues back to San Francisco, up to Seattle, and all the way back east, I am satisfied the pueo have my back and those of my family. I may not see around the bend, but I feel cared for with each step. I hold the pueo to their word until they fulfill their covenant and until such time as I hear a voice from the heavenly end of a white tunnel announce, "You have arrived."

On Earth, water is my way of life. It beckons me, it sustains me, and it drowns me. It is my blessing and my curse.

When I reach Nebraska and the skies grow dark once more, the scales tilt undeniably towards cursing. As I change into my eleventh pair of shoes, I remember that it's easiest to see candle-light in darkness.

In an Elm Creek, Nebraska, Pump N Go gas station,
Farmer Daryl reminisces about his cowboy father as
he and Paula share coffee while
staying out of the Nebraskan rain on
July 10, 2019 at 7,894 miles during
Leg 16 of the Happiness Walk.

IT'S NOT FOR EVERYONE

This is the most rain I've ever seen in my life, and I'm eighty-nine.
It's the most rain I've ever heard of around here.

—Daryl

Elm Creek, Nebraska

Kimo has assured me my lifespan will exceed a full century. Even if true, I can't imagine recreating an experience the likes of this Happiness Walk.

I maneuvered my way through several sketchy scenarios during this venture. Coyotes tracked my scent as I was wedged between a high embankment in Oregon, a highway, and barbed fencing. I performed the Heimlich maneuver on a fellow walker choking on chili made by our startled host in Georgia, I received an incoming-missile message while walking the streets of Oahu. And most extraordinary, I outwitted pit bulls. But as is apparent, I survived. And thanks to mandatory training in first aid several decades back, so did my fellow chili eater. After a quick cleanup, we finished our meal in deference to our host. I vowed to myself I would never eat chili again.

Walking is rarely a cliff hanger. It is, however, seductive. So, one must be careful with the lure of seduction and where it might lead.

I've met adversity, and I've challenged my physical self to the far reaches of a sixty-something's fitness bell curve. On more than one occasion, death nipped at my heels. Still, the cumulative strife never eclipses the intoxication of the walkabout. Rather, it enhances it.

"Life is a discovery," says Jared Long of Lincoln, Nebraska. "There's a lot in the world that is easy to feel concerned or be negative about. But you have to focus on that sometimes, because you have to discover the problems to fix the problems."

It's ironic that I take that particular opportunity to quote a Nebraskan.

"Paula, what's the place you enjoyed walking through the most?" asks everyone.

Like those who respond to my question in the negative, I quip like a smart ass, "Not Nebraska."

But if I'm honest with myself, Nebraska floats to the top of a flood of memories. In part, a literal flood makes it so memorable.

Bridges down, streets damaged, topsoil stripped from its farmland, and the ground satiated from two years of heavy rains surround me as I slosh my way through Cornhusker country during the summer of 2019. I cross a time zone and a state line from Julesburg, Colorado, into Nebraska in late June and arrive in North Platte on the third of July—just in time to celebrate the founding of the country—not with the traditional barrage of fireworks but with blinding bursts of lightning.

Fourth of July, 2019
41.1403°N, 100.7601°W
North Platte, Nebraska

Concerned it might lift into orbit with me as its passenger, I flee my leaky, wind-swept tent. Better it soars on its own. I dodge lightning and sheets of rain to take cover in the cinder-block shower stall at the Holiday Park and RV Campground in North

Platte. In a reverse riff on typical lightning storms, total darkness briefly blasts through ceaseless electrical strikes. Soaked, tired, and frightened, I dare a short run to an all-night diner where I purchase a dry t-shirt to absorb a small portion of chill from my bones. I order hot coffee and a cup of chili, both of them served lukewarm and topped off with crippling food poisoning.

Twelve hours later, my gear hung out to dry on every available surface of my clean and reasonably priced motel room, I lay sprawled on the bathroom floor and admonish myself for faulting on my chili promise. Between bouts of violent vomiting, I contemplate quitting the walk. I've had fleeting thoughts before, of course, but I never really meant them.

I'm tired.

I'm discouraged.

The room is spinning, and I am so alone.

And I'm in goddamned Nebraska!

However, time brings sleep and, with it, a renewed perspective as it usually does. I awake with more resolve, but first I need a hot cup of coffee. As I pass the Cappuccino and Steamers restaurant on my way out of town, I gag and affirm I will never have the impulse to return to Nebraska ever again.

Honestly, it's not for everyone is the state's new tourism motto ironically created by a Colorado ad agency. To be clear, it's a rallying cry meant to attract tourism, but even some Nebraskans question its sentiment which seems to say, "Walk on by." It's akin to promoting an all-night diner by saying "Our food is often hot. Most people don't get sick after they eat our chili." Still, some Nebraskans are quite proud of their slogan, which asserts that their home state is not an acquired taste—you either love it or don't, and no one is offended if you leave.

Five days later, the road out of Lexington is closed. Route 30 is two feet under water from seven inches of overnight rain, with all access to it blocked. I am headed to Kearney where everyone in the entire southeast portion of the city must evacuate. I stand at a literal crossroads, my backpack already digging into my shoulders because the supporting straps can no longer adjust to my thinning hips. The unrelenting strain causes dull, persistent nausea.

My body needs a rest.

I flag down a passing sheriff and convince him to give me a ride through the flooded street and drop me off when pavement returns. I hadn't counted on additional flooding up ahead with cars abandoned on either side of the road and others immersed in water. Household yards have given way to rivers, and pets find refuge on garage roofs. Though the day is hot and the going slow, I manage to make it the twenty miles to Elm Creek.

It seems each rural town welcomes me into its fold from long corridors of corn. Nebraska doesn't differ much from Colorado except stalks stand a little taller since leaving Denver. I will eventually walk the full seed, growth, and harvest cycles of corn over the length of the current leg of the walk. Somehow, I will miss the eating phase.

From a distance on the straight, flat roads, I see the telltale signs of town: a long row of tall adjoining grain silos and a water tank on its highest point. Nearly all towns I'm walking through dot the railroad tracks running east and west.

I love the moment right before I approach a new place. Each community appears a carbon copy of the previous one but with its own unique flavor, and I can't wait to get a taste. I immediately seek out the obligatory gathering place—a gas station, grocery store, coffeeshop, or restaurant. It is rare they are not one and the same. If I'm really lucky, I find a bowling alley that serves bar food with Keno on the side. Another faction of the town gathers where the conversation flows as warmly as the beer.

I brave 108 degrees in full sun, so I arrive sweaty with half a golfer's tan. In other words, my right side gets painted by the sun more than my left, and I wear permanent farmer-tanned white socks when barefoot. The drinking water I carry is too hot to drink, so I'm eager to get a cold beverage and emphatically repeat the promise never ever again to take ice for granted.

So many promises.

Once I address my thirst, I sit down with a coffee to get the lay of the land, usually from a semi-retired farmer meeting his semi-retired farmer friends to discuss the health of their crops, topsoil erosion of their fields, or condition of their equipment. A new face in town is rather an anomaly—especially a woman with a backpack—so I garner a bit of attention.

Today I meet Daryl and friends.

"No, there's no place other than the Pump N Go to eat in town."

"Yes, there is a recreation field down that road on your right by the pool."

"This place opens at dawn with coffee and hot breakfast pizza." "What matters, most? Well, let me tell you, Little Girl . . . " I've gone from Baby to Sugar to Honey to Ms. Paula and now to Little Girl. It seems I'm sometimes reverse-aging as the years pass. I wait out the light by the pool then find a discreet spot to camp under the town's pavilion to keep me dry from inevitable evening lightning storms. My bad-ass attitude keeps me grounded, and a strong desire to get through the state keeps me making miles.

The state's new slogan replaced *Nebraska Nice*. I believe both are apropos. After just seven days and already looking forward to leaving the state, it's clear to me nothing can water down the good nature of its people. Kearney proves my point.

Unsure of my next move since a good part of the town is still under water and the ground is too wet for tenting, I immediately seek out a restaurant. I learn the flooding isn't going away. It's simply retreating east along my route, so again, the road is closed. Kitt's Kitchen and Coffee, however, offers an oasis in a string of Pump N Gos. The food is heavenly, the coffee is strong, and the people are generous with their interest and time. There I meet Jeena and Kathryn. Without much apparent thought, they invite me to dinner at Kathryn's and offer me a bed at Jeena and her husband, Brett's. Without much apparent thought, I accept.

As James Jenkins of Cerro Gorda, South Carolina, says, "Land is land, but the people make the difference." Friendly, curious, engaging, and honest, the people of the soggy place blow my white socks off. People wear their pride in their community like the compulsory cowboy hats on their heads and revel in moments of its glory.

I hear stories of love and stories of pain. I learn of devastating events made tolerable only through the fellowship of family and neighbors. I walk in awe of how history is ingrained in each day, how ancestors are never that far away, and how the cutting-edge future comingles with the past. Best of all, Nebraskans' dish out laughter in generous portions—a skill I admire and lust after.

Kathryn and her husband, Kendall, serve salad with Dorothy Lynch dressing (a Nebraskan thing), garden-fresh vegetables, farm-raised pork, and canned stewed peaches, all direct from their farm in a small town south of Kearney. I appreciate being close to my food source, and I surely am that in the heartlands and elsewhere around the country's arable landscape.

Throughout the walk, I bypass fields of peanuts and cotton in the South, fruits and vegetables in the West, soy and, of course, corn in the heartlands. I smell the riches of grapes in New York, apples in Washington, and cilantro in California. I relish the abundant beauty of sunflowers, pumpkins, and wheat fields. Oysters, asparagus, pineapples, crawfish, green beans, avocados, persimmons, lettuce, melons, coffee beans and on and on . . . I've walked through them all.

But nothing can compare to the local delicacies: boiled peanuts, beignets, Rocky Mountain oysters, poutine, etouffee, tamales, pralines, boiled lobster, Dorothy Lynch Home Style Dressing and Condiment, and so much more. I get to explore many ethnic preparations as well: Creole, Italian, Mexican, Chinese, Cajun, Greek, Indian—oh my! It is a good thing the walk requires ten hours of daily physical activity! You can easily say I have eaten my way around the country. And for my troubles, I've collected a few memorable recipes I hope someday to recreate in my own future kitchen.

To be sure, it takes arduous effort to put food on our tables. "Farming is really, really hard work. Working around animals and soil is hard on one's body," confides Tom Dixon of La Cienega, New Mexico. The grueling work etches itself in the hands I shake and in the creases of faces I greet. I observe how growers work the fields from early in the morning until late into the evening. Not many people can afford to live such a life, and I worry about what that means for our future plates.

We must consider the gravity of soil quality on the health of the farming industry. As Kurt Pipa of Ithaca, New York, reminds me, soil is largely a byproduct of millions of years of rock erosion. It is "part of the ecosystem—something that's alive, even though it seems like a dead thing." Kurt's passion for soil health has him raising black soldier flies in his home which are used for clean and efficient composting purposes. He teaches me we can improve the nutritional value of foods through cultivation of soil, the living epidermis of our land. I never before considered harvesting soil like we harvest peas and carrots, but Kurt's explanation makes great sense. With that new information, I hope there are enough black soldier flies for the depleted fields of Nebraska.

It's not soldier flies I find on Nebraskan roads, though. "The mosquitoes aren't as bad as the gnats—and then there are the flying cockroaches," someone complains to me in North Carolina. Apparently, that person never met Nebraska horse flies. It will take me twenty-two days to traverse the state, all the while swatting the large insects from my sweaty face and bare limbs. That's twenty days too long. I never knew how severely and frequently those blackguards sting. I later learn it's because, rather than simply piercing your skin as does a polite, well-mannered bee, the mouth parts of horse flies tear at your skin like a great white shark attacking a poor, innocent seal.

I spend eleven nights tenting in recreation fields mined with water spigots that discharge after dark. No matter how I try to outsmart them, I always wake up wet, followed by as many nights drying out gear in a cheap hotel or a host's guest room. I spend several days wading through flooded streets. I eat too much bowling-alley fries, get a super-sized tan on my right side, swat at horse flies, and chomp on as much ice as I can get my hands on.

On the other hand, I love the smell of freshly rolled haystacks and manure sprayed on fields. I suppose it hearkens back to living most of my adult life in Vermont, which purportedly has more cows than people.

Some exceptionally friendly and generous hosts also bless my time in the state.

Nebraskans deserve their slogans. And though I will tell and retell stories of the Cornhusker state until I die, you may have guessed—Nebraska is not for me.

As I reflect on Jared's call to "discover the problems to fix the problems," I wonder how many waves of disasters a place can weather before the tides of resilience forever turn and futures drown. We humans face many storms, and as Jared points out, we must digest their causes and purge them if we are to heal.

Life certainly is a discovery, and we discover new solutions every day. We raise black soldier flies. We suspend staircases in mid air. We survive being buried alive. We put one foot in front of the other after a couple of dark days. We are innovative, resourceful, and scrappy.

And, thank goodness, some of us have humor.

Had I not weathered storms, injuries and illnesses, isolation and loneliness, and grief and despair, I would not have the depth of empathy required to listen fully to all the people who gave of themselves so selflessly to the Happiness Walk and to me. Listening without judgment is the twin sister to living without fear. My non judgment was fashioned in Vermont and affirmed in Hawaii but honed in the heartlands.

Ah . . . Nebraska.

Once again, a state starts out with a bang. This time, thankfully, the bang turns into a blessing. All of it—each unpredictable soggy moment—I wholeheartedly welcomed.

Of course, I say that only once I reach Iowa.

*Rain cascades on the horizon of
Paula's eastward journey in Maybell, Colorado, on
June 1, 2019, at 7,312 miles during
Leg 16 of the Happiness Walk.*

RAIN, RAIN GO AWAY

Wildness equals happiness.

—Laurel

Barnard, Vermont

I am exhausted much of the time. I expect I would sleepwalk my way through the day if the road weren't so interesting. But it is. Everything is stimulating and new.

May 30, 2019
40.2436°N, 109.0146°W
Dinosaur, Colorado

Light streams in and I awake, but I won't yet open my eyes. I don't want to. Even with my winter hat on and nose tucked into my sleeping bag, I can feel intense cold creeping in to freeze-dry me and the contents of my tent.

I eventually muster the will to unzip my covers and start packing. I organize as much as I can while still in my bag as I deflate the mattress beneath me, letting my weight squeeze the air from its lungs. Slow lowering to the cold hard ground suffices to kick me into high gear. As quietly as I can, I place my things into my hip pack and backpack—everything in its proper place. If I move it, I lose it.

Someday I will be able to stay in bed—a real bed, a warm mattress—and sleep until I'm rested. That possibility seems like eons away, since I still have six months before the next scheduled break.

I didn't sleep well last night under the pavilion at the town park. It sits right on the highway, and swings and a dinosaur-shaped slide attracted families with young children well into the evening. The adjacent lot hosted truckers who kept their engines running all night.

In the growing dark, my tent was less than stealthy when the automatic pavilion lights flashed on just as I closed my eyes. I managed to find an off switch, but it took just enough energy to keep me awake for another hour.

The sun arrived too quickly. After brushing my teeth behind a bush with water from my pack, I find a bathroom, a hot egg and cheese sandwich, and coffee across the street at the Loaf 'N Jug convenience store and gas station. Open twenty-four seven, it, too, generated endless headlights and slammed doors throughout the evening. This particular small town with 339 residents has more activity than Best Buy on Black Friday.

It doesn't matter where on the map this town sits, the story repeats itself morning after morning, state after state. Luckily, breakfast options increase with the population, but nightly accommodations stay pretty much the same with an unsuspected floodlight, lawn sprinkler, or critter to keep me from my dreams.

In the half mile it takes me to get out of town, I pass three cannabis dispensaries, perhaps another reason for the heavy traffic. Dinosaur, Colorado, sits just three miles inside the state border from Utah, a less-imbibing state—or at least once a less-dispensing one since medical marijuana became legal just six months before. Cautiously, I watch cars that share the same side of the street, although it's the ones leaving town I suspect invite more concern. It takes some time before the stench of roadkill overtakes the skunky smell of pot.

Depending on the wind, the funk of a rotting carcass warns me well in advance of the source, time enough to raise my kerchief to my nose for several hundred feet. I don't always see the poor creatures, but I know when I've moved past. On one sad occasion, I found a pet dog and called the owner's number on the collar to give her the bad news. She did not sound as perturbed as I, and I hated the idea of him alone. That is also how I see the only bighorn sheep of the walk but even more tragically and horrifyingly, a horse's head. Still, I am unprepared when I happen across a forensic team attending a washed-up human body on the Pacific Coast or when a Florida news station reports on a dead human body I unknowingly brushed past the day before.

There it is again—death: the circle of life, ever present and unavoidable.

But so, too, is life. And its opposite reminds me to be grateful for its bounty.

Sensory gifts bestowed upon me daily include the stillness of Keechelus Lake in Washington that mirrors dusty blue mountains. Tumbleweed blows across the corridor by a distant storm dancing in the Texas heavens, orange and yellow sunsets drop from New Mexico hills, enormous and majestic trunks of the Redwoods root in California, and the ancient Angel Tree Live Oak kneels so gracefully to the ground in Georgia.

Antelopes leap, dolphins jump, eagles circle, prairie dogs pop, and tarantulas crawl on roads, in fields, in oceans, in skies, through corn. The cacophony of crows, peeps of toads, whinnies of wild horses, pounding of waves on shores, in trees, across hills, under fronds—all comprise instruments of life's musical ensemble.

Then there's the ubiquitous sound of wind as it whispers through the trees—a sound with a name: psithurism. We all know the sound even if we don't know the name. It accompanies us wherever breezes blow. It's the soft murmur of air against the sway of greens and browns. Psithurism. If you say it slowly, it mimics the sigh of creation, nature's secret language.

As I move my body, my heart pumps questions to my mind. I contemplate the breadth of what's visible—how much goes unseen I could nevertheless observe. I wonder what I fail to perceive through nature's inherent masking of light and sound. I wish to be privy to it all.

"And now here is my secret, a very simple secret," I recall the fox saying to the Little Prince, "it is only with the heart that one can see rightly. What is essential is invisible to the eye." So I stay attentive and avoid the exhaustion of plodding through slumber. I listen for the psithurism I compose as I give sway to my mellifluous wanderings.

Not atypically, the world synthesizes according to my wishes.

Tax Day 2018
44.0313°N, 123.8595°W
Mapleton, Oregon

Sometimes rain is so wet. Like Forrest Gump, I have walked in every kind of rain. Today, it rains for the sixteenth day in a row. Following the Siuslaw River, I turn east towards Eugene and wade along the Oregon coast. Light misting turns into torrents roaring from the blackening sky. Day after day it drenches my bones and percolates through my nerves.

Peering from under my flapping red umbrella, I see only slivers of road. A thunderstorm threatens but not close enough to dampen my stride. Wind jostles me off the shoulder. Its strength breaks the spokes of my umbrella just before it breaks my spirits.

Before I go further, and to provide a sense of my reaction, I must return a full month to Ukiah, California, again in rain, and on that fifteenth day in March, also hail.

The precipitation doesn't daunt me, and I even love the way hail makes rivers down the hill to Ukiah's City of Ten Thousand Buddhas. A golden arched gateway on Bodhi Way invites visitors to walk the much longer Buddhist Middle Way. Just past Kindness Avenue sits the community's administrative offices. An interview gets me a coveted answer to my high level questions, "Why?" and "How?"

The answer I receive from the brown-robed monk? "Shit happens."

I find the meditation hall between Avatamsaka and Giving ways, lined with ten thousand golden Buddhas of all dimensions and reflect on his profound answer before I find my way to downtown.

I've heard good things about Ukiah and am eager to get there—until I arrive. I am unable to discern reasons for the buzz. I am soaked through and don't find a patch of dry grass around, so I secure a room at the closest Motel 6 right next to Sunny's Donuts. I pass a busy bus stop on my way there, and I meet John and Cheri.

"It's not money," answers John to my customary question. He calls himself a transient and drug addict who attempted to hang himself under a local bridge on his most recent birthday.

"Don't define yourself," inserts Cheri as she sifts through the trash can. "Don't let him get away with that," she directs me. "God matters. And money isn't evil. It's how people worship it."

"Lady," she adds, "this town is full of homeless people. It attracts the homeless because of all the services they have here."

That looks correct from my practiced perspective.

When I leave, John shakes my hand, "Good to talk and be listened to. One stranger to another, I promise I'll quit drugging." As a person living in the same grove, I pray he receives the nourishment he lacks.

The next day's route takes me on a highway with construction I avoid by detouring to a hilly bypass through woods scorched by one of the more recent fires. The bypass ends in a four-foot barrier. Shooting Range reads the sign.

I jump the fence and strut on as if I belong. Thankfully, the fence has an opening about three miles and several muted gunshots later just beyond a tree downed across my lane by the previous day's storm. I make my way over and through the debris as the owner of the private property greets me while he continues to chop wood. He asks no questions and kindly hands me his card so I can call in case I ever get into trouble.

Cars linger in ditches due to snow that accumulated after the hail, but I make it safely back to Motel 6 where I stay a second night—but wish I hadn't.

"I want my momma," I hear a young boy cry to an unsympathetic woman. There's a young girl, too. The walls are thin, and I hear the children whimper as the woman vehemently scolds them.

There's commotion throughout the night in that room next to mine. A man bangs on my neighbor's door around 2 AM.

"Let me in, bitch." They scream at each other. He slams the door, leaves, and returns banging and yelling two hours later.

The children cry.

What the hell?

I try to catch a glimpse of the man as he leaves the room or of the vehicle he drives. Nothing. I pack up early and sit at the doughnut counter where I can observe the motel for activity.

Nothing.

I'm too late. I didn't approach them, so I have little to report to authorities except for my suspicions that the children should not be with those people. I'm convinced something is wholly rotten. My stomach is sour.

Later that day, shaken to my core, I call my sister Pam, who informs me of the child trafficking route I am walking. I feel it. The ground quakes beneath me. The place feels dark and evil. Misty gray clouds pass as the only visible colors that can penetrate its abyss.

The truth of what I witnessed seems to reveal itself in hindsight. I cannot forgive myself for my lack of acumen to take action. I stagnate in that cloud for numberless days. Rain continues to cry, as do I.

Back in Oregon, I've had it! I cannot any longer withstand the dankness of my innards. The moisture from my eyes is indistinguishable from the beads of rain leaking to my chest.

I stop. I weakly drop my broken umbrella. Passing cars splash buckets of tears onto my person.

I scream. I throw the gauntlet down and yell to God, "Do you want me? Do you really want to test me more? Then come get me! I'm right here! Give me what you've got! You're not going to beat me! I've got this! I win!"

Hours later, fingers numb and lips purple, I release an emotional river on the floor with each squeaking step down the aisles of a grocery store where I purchase a new umbrella. I sit in my dampness with a coffee and a satisfying insight that I won!

The following day it rains.

I receive the refreshing gift that showers the stench from my being. It cleanses me—body, mind, and spirit. Lightning bolts animate the sky, and I dance to the rumbling music from heaven.

I am not asleep.

Ahh . . . this is what freedom is!

After two hours of slow moving in the inky dampness of
Snoqualmie Tunnel in Hyak, Washington, Paula emerges victorious on
July 28, 2018, at 6,124 miles during
Leg 14 of the Happiness Walk.

ONE TOE IN THE GROUND

There's something inside all of us as human beings.
We fill the void with a lot of different things, but I think there's such
satisfaction in giving to someone else; there's more reward and
enjoyment in giving than receiving.

—Captain Rob Hecocks
Los Gatos, California

As I write, all hell breaks loose. Nothing is as it was during the seven years of the Happiness Walk. Mere providence permitted me to finish the full ten thousand miles just months before a pandemic shut the world down and all manner of mayhem ensued.

I am very grateful (for completing the walk, not for the mayhem).

However the world looks as I type away, I predict the slow drip of that chaos will have amplified into a raging torrent with the aging of these words. An optimist, I also predict the chaos will lead us to something better. We won't secure new systems if we build them over the distortion of existing ones. We must dismantle our old structures before we can erect new ones on solid foundations. What we build—where we take the story—is up to each of us.

How we get there is also up to us. I find fear unhelpful and debilitating. I prefer the advice of Bryan Hall, executive director of Eureka, California, Rescue Mission. Once incarcerated, he has embarked on helping fellow addicts recover from their dependencies.

"When things are chaotic and life is upside down," he said, "I imagine myself like a piece of wood in a stream, and I just float. I may go under, I may catch an eddy, but nevertheless, I still come back up, and I'm able to keep floating. I'm always making progress. I'm always moving forward."

July 28, 2018
47.3923°N, 121.4001°W
Snoqualmie Pass, Washington

I collapse into a vinyl and Formica beige and brown booth set on a checkerboard floor at iconic Twedes's Café, also known as Double R Diner, in North Bend, Washington. ABC filmed a portion of the television series *Twin Peaks* at Twedes. I never saw the entire show, but apparently a *Twin Peaks* resident acts characteristically unique and quirky. If true, I feel at home—minus the theatrics. The dramatic Cascade Mountains tower over the town as gatekeepers to the dense Douglas Firs at their backs. My steps take me there next, and I need to figure out how best to transit the daunting mountains.

As I review my options over a slice of pie and a damned fine cup of coffee, I sketch out a two-day, unconventional route along wooded mountain trails and an old railroad bed to Cle Elum. That route will circumvent dangerous hairpin turns on Interstate 90, although it also involves steep climbing, bear habitation, and a 2.253-mile-long tunnel.

Towards the end of the first day, flashlight in hand, I approach Snoqualmie Tunnel for what I perceive to be a forty-five-minute undertaking. There's a slight curve to the passageway that denies entrance to light from the opposite end. Once I venture past the first bend, the pinpoint of light behind me succumbs to complete blackness.

No motorized traffic is allowed in the tunnel. Only an occasional bicycle or rare group of walkers with headlamps pass by. No one walks alone—except for me.

It is ninety degrees outside, but tunnel air feels chilly and damp. Condensation drips from every pore of every stone to form puddles of sweat on the pock-marked floor.

Drip. Plop. Drip. A metallic aftertaste lingers on the back of my tongue.

Each echoing step ricochets off drooling walls and vacuous unseen spaces, and the entirety appears weeping for its lost usefulness.

Crunch. Drip. Plop.

My flashlight proves anemic against the inky force. My fingertips are numb and my mind silent. I suck in the heavy, musty air held captive in a chamber carved deep through the terrain's rocky outcropping, and I couple my gait to the exceedingly slow and steady rhythm of droplets that pierce the dark and measure time.

Drip. Crunch. Plop.

Brrr.

I love every unfolding minute of the alive and exhilarating netherworld! I breathe out a desire for more.

Darkness rises to challenge my courage, but it's no match for my resolve. I slowly and steadfastly forge my way forward through the eye of the needle.

Two surprising hours later, I step into a blast of bright summer heat, remove my gloves, don my sunglasses, and bask in the feat I have sown.

And here we are, together at the eye of another needle.

"It's a funny thing," writes Khaled Hosseini in *And the Mountains Echoed*. "People mostly have it backwards. They think they live by what they want. But what guides them is what they're afraid of."

Worry is a fervent prayer for what we don't want. I'd rather respond to the urging of the Reverend William Barber, "We are called to be the thermostats that change the temperature, not the thermostat that merely *tells* the temperature."

If you believe the fabric of our times to be dark, I urge you to get out your flashlight. While I could not see but a few feet in front of me, I knew my next steps would reveal the next few feet and a few more after that.

We don't have to see the end of the tunnel to know it is there. Even through necessary razing of old and outdated systems, we can find solace in the ground under our shoes, although transitions often require we straddle both old and new until someone or something lays hopeful tracks for our travels. I recently came across a sustainable development framework I believe reflects what people say they value. Coincidentally, Kate Raworth terms it Doughnut Economics—now that's something I can sink my teeth into and so appropriate for the Happiness Walk.

Doughnut Economics resembles a Gross National Happiness model in that people's needs and livelihoods are the doughnut hole of—or fundamental to—our decision-making. Maintained within the boundaries of an ecological outer crust, a delicious regenerative economy surrounds the hole. While Ms. Raworth's model does not include subjective measures, it stresses the need to live respectfully within our planetary boundaries. I believe we have the ingredients for such a plan. We only need the will to make it work.

There it is again: the will.

Creative new systems require our conscious attention and our intention. As we strive for important goals we hold dear, we must also design communities that align with what we value and desire. We need a new diet that banishes fear, isolation, scarcity, and dependency that has been whisked into every morsel of our lives.

What is before us is what we've cultivated. We must either endure it and possibly die from it, or we will learn and move on to transform our lives and, thus, our planet. As President John F. Kennedy said in 1963, "This country cannot afford to be materially rich and spiritually poor." I fiercely believe we must, with a sense of urgency, explore our elegant world with hearts wide open and with our lights shining brightly.

That's how Pure Freakin' Magic shows itself.

Today
1.58 x 10-5 light years from Sol
the Orion Arm of Milky Way Galaxy
8.178 0.035 Kiloparsecs from the Galactic Center
Earth

The white band of flesh on my left ring finger starkly reminds me of just how much has changed since I took my first steps. I have come to rely on freshly manifested crutches of self-sufficiency, self-reliance, self-acceptance, purpose, and resiliency—all stuffed into my psychological backpack.

Quite honestly, I'd be hard pressed to name anything that hasn't changed since I began the walk. Physically, I feel younger and more energetic. My nails grow faster, and my feet are wider. My hair, where it isn't gray, bleached from dark brown to blonde due to excessive sun exposure. Even the color of my eyes has morphed, and I certainly see things differently. Each cell in our bodies rejuvenates every seven years, so I am quite literally not the same person I was when I started.

Of course, other body parts are wrinkling, spotting, and sagging to my knees. I require reading glasses to see the GPS and quiet spaces to use the phone. My metabolism has gone haywire. Each time I returned home between legs of the walk, I easily and deliciously put on pounds, comfortable in ceremoniously fattening up like a Thanksgiving turkey for the next stretch of a long, hard walk. But, alas, the time has come when I no longer need such athletic reserves, and my pants are irrefutably protesting.

Intellectually, I have always been a curious person, so my education continues to grow about random and not-so-random subjects: happiness (of course), archeology and alchemy (fascinating), mysticism and quantum physics (which I suggest are related), the history of mankind and alien encounters (perhaps also related), economics, geometry, parallel universes, time travel, and what makes us human.

There are an infinite number of questions to ponder on and off the road. But my most weighty inquiry has always been on the subject of the self, my self. Who am I? What am I? Why am I? I am left with an infinite and growing number of questions even after many miles of silent reflection.

I have unwaveringly learned that I refuse to fall back into my emotional habit of needing to feel loved in an attempt to define who I am. That truly would be time travel. A recent tarot reading counsels me to "relinquish all contracts except that which contributes to the power of my living." When I next love, I promise myself to stand in my ultimate Goddess-given power and tell doubt and fear to go take a hike—without me!

In the end, I'd like to think I've grown at the deepest core of my being and that my light within shines a little more powerfully and brilliantly after a lifetime of spiritual seeking, years of active listening, and days of meditative walking. Who really knows? Once I think I know something, it's time to bear down on its truth, so, I'm leaving the sum of my spiritual development as a definite open question.

One last story about me. I am reluctant to tell it and have kept it quiet for many years. Nevertheless, vulnerable as I am, I will share it. I think it may have relevance regarding our futures.

I was five years old when I stood at the window with my sister Pam. Our younger sister Chris slept soundly in the corner of our small bedroom. What I saw that night shaped the rest of my life.

A large swirling, blinking, oblong object hovered in my backyard. As with the mountain lion and the one-eyed owl, I sensed a familiar respect. I looked at it and it at me for an indeterminate period of time until its curiosity was satisfied. (Mine still is not!) Leaving an indelible mark on my psyche, it swept away with lightning speed just as portrayed by many who've shared such an experience.

I lost that memory and turned it into a dream. Even with my mother's endless search for cosmic intelligence, it still didn't resurface. It wasn't until much later, when as an adult I shared my dream with Pam, that I knew it was not imagined nor an apparition. It's no wonder I have searched for truth throughout my life. I understand the gravity of this carnal existence. I have an abiding reverence for our time here, and I yearn to understand the workings of the universe to make sense of our collective cosmic voyage.

What I can see is that life is expansive. Its possibilities are greater than what I know and will know in this lifetime. Where truth resides is beyond my reach. So, as I reflect upon lessons I've learned while walking and writing and reflecting and wondering and observing and appreciating, I am only tapping into the wisdom afforded me in the moment. That is the best any of us can do: test, test, test our beliefs and hold them up to the light, find our individual proof, walk our individual path.

So, that is how I persevere in talking about happiness, even though, for many, life hasn't been an easy journey. I'm not sure it was meant to be. However, I do believe each of us is meant to experience joy—to live in joy.

I suggest now is the time to cultivate happiness, perhaps more ardently than ever. Happiness is not simply a feeling state that puts a smile on your face. Happiness is the essence of our whole being—or holy being. It encompasses all that brings goodness into life. We are traveling sacred soil. Together and with purpose, we can simultaneously bear witness to the turbulence and float to calmer shores as we walk in balance with Mother Earth and bow to the wisdom in one another.

Because of my experiences, I've had the luxury of learning how to step into the unknown and am comfortable with the uncertainty of life as I consider my mother's routine forewarning, "Know that you don't know." I have a long history of schooling in an openness to the unknowable. But let's face it, it took me walking around the country to get it through my thick skull! I am here to say you don't have to scale the mountains, traverse the deserts, or crisscross the states to unearth important lessons.

"The ideals we hold don't come for free," suggests Seth Ricker, my host in the town of Fieldbrook, California, for two nights. "Everybody says they want a healthy environment, loving connections, peace, and a spiritually-grounded society. But then when push comes to shove, it's not for free, right? So, we have to say, 'This is important to us. We're going to make it important in all our decisions we make in our lives.'"

The price, I believe, is the dissolution of fear. We don't need to know where our next steps will lead us, only that solid ground will find us. Trust that everything will work out—differently than we anticipate perhaps, but in my experience, better than we can imagine. As John Lennon said, "Everything will be okay in the end. If it's not okay, it's not the end."

That feels true, because the tunnel bends towards the light.

We the People matter! So, assuming what I've learned from a multitude of teachers I met along the way may be of value to others on their own journeys, I share what I regard as truths laboriously earned:

Pursue your passions despite what others may think.

Be curious and discerning.

Serve others.

Trust your wisdom and paint life's canvas with unique expressions of your being.

Love with your whole heart.

Earnestly and genuinely forgive yourself and others.

Feed your happiness dog.

Release insistence on outcomes to allow for manifestation of miracles.

Forever keep one toe in the ground as you reach for your highest and noble, starry potential.

As I traveled up the Pacific Coast, I became familiar with the story of salmon. My host Seth, an expert on the subject at the US Department of Fish and Wildlife, explained how salmon are woven into the fabric of the Northwest. "From the native cultures to European settlers, up to now, the landscape is host to salmon and the ocean is part of salmon. It's how people identify with history, with culture, with the environment." It is also how people relate to their ancestors.

Salmon of the Pacific Northwest are world-renowned. They are anadromous fish, meaning they are born in freshwater then migrate out to the ocean to mature into adults. Trusting their internal GPSes, they navigate a return to freshwater to spawn in the exact stream where they were born. Nature being what it is, most adults die after spawning and their decaying carcasses render nutrients back into the ecosystem, providing nourishment for other life forms in a way similar to the aspen.

Based on teachings handed down by the elders in Choctaw, Lakota, Seneca, Aztec, Yaqui, Cheyenne, Cherokee, Iroquois, and Mayan traditions, the shamans David Carson and Jamie Sams offer the following insight into salmon medicine for the nourishment of humanity.

"Salmon are sacred keepers of wisdom and inner knowing whose sense of purpose cannot be thwarted by external forces. Coming full circle, salmon medicine people finish what they begin, bringing life's events and cycles to closure."

Perhaps or even probably, you and I are salmon people. I believe we have chosen to walk together at this particular time on Earth. If so, the responsibility for ending the discordant cycle of disharmony and to spawn the new and heavenly dawn of peace falls to us.

During a visit to my sister Pam's in Puerto Escondido, Mexico, I waded into the ocean up to my chest. The waves were just high enough to enjoy body surfing. With my back to the open water, ready to catch the next wave, my eyes caught Pam on the beach waving her arms frantically. I couldn't hear what she screamed, but I intuited enough to turn around.

A rogue wave licked my back. I could do nothing but fall into acceptance. As seconds passed, I made my peace with drowning. The monster stole my feet and placed them above my head. Up was down, down was up. Time inched by. I somersaulted in slow motion like wet laundry surrendering to the drum of the dryer—round and round, flopping limbs and twisting torso.

Buddhist tradition emphasizes the natural and inevitable appearance of death. A common Buddhist metaphor involves the symbolism of waves as explained by Chidi to Eleanor in the TV series *The Good Place,* my guilty pleasure during a worldwide quarantine in 2020.

"Picture a wave in the ocean. You can see it, measure it, its height, the way the sunlight refracts when it passes through, and it's there, and you can see it, you know what it is. It's a wave. And then it crashes on the shore, and it's gone. But the water is still there. The wave was just a different way for the water to be for a little while. The wave returns to the ocean, where it came from, and where it's supposed to be."

As the wave carried me, I heard a whisper of guidance from a distant voice. Remain calm. Do not struggle. Swim parallel to the beach, not toward it. I listened, and the next wave guided me to safety. Why the ocean didn't claim me then, I do not know. Gasping for air, I was instead anchored to the living by several pounds of sand in my suit stripped to my knees—a humbling sight.

So I live to witness most extraordinary times where waitress Brenda's hell is breaking loose and we from it. Wise counsel tells us to remain calm even though the currents of change are strong. Salmon tell us to listen to our inner GPS and not give into distractions nor the detours and roadblocks of outer conditions. With perseverance, we will get to the other side.

What remains after the wave breaks may just be the very thing for which we have been praying.

I met Eva in Taos, New Mexico. She brought the following with her from Poland: "You carry your happiness in your own backpack."

I leave the following with you.

With a commitment of intention out to the universe, may we willfully navigate the living waters as a salmon—born of spirit, awash with wisdom, and carrying our own backpacks of happiness.

As for me, well, the walk was just one way for me to be for a while.

ACKNOWLEDGEMENTS

Choosing stories for *18 Pair of Shoes* compares closely with choosing between water and air. Ultimately, I had to decide which best support the story I had to tell—even then, I might have included many more.

My selections don't diminish the significance of all the people not mentioned who confided in me, nurtured and nourished me, walked with me, financially contributed, or otherwise supported me along the Happiness Walk. I remember you for your many kindnesses from routes you suggested to save me miles of relief from pavement to power drinks that quenched my thirst on hot sunny days. I remember you for many pounds of gifts bestowed upon me, hundreds of beds I slept in, rides received from those willing to pick up an unknown woman at the side of the road in an era not friendly to hitchhikers, and food—oh, the food.

Most especially to the thousands of people whose conversations I recorded or didn't record, thank you for your accommodation, thoughtfulness, and candor. I hope you enjoyed our talks as much as I cherish them, even the ones accomplished through stalls in public restrooms—those fall into the unrecorded category.

While you opened your hearts and doors to me, I held back much of myself in order to maintain the unbiased nature of the walk project. Nevertheless, you gave so much to me—you offered me experiences and lessons that have changed me forever.

I am endlessly grateful to each and every one of you.

The many gifts offered me by my sister Christine Noyes made the arduous effort of writing a book exponentially easier. After completing the Happiness Walk, I had no home to return to, no car to drive, no job to retreat into. On top of that, my laptop crashed while I was walking. Chris graciously provided me that and more as I slowly and selectively added material goods back into my life and acclimated to off-road living.

Then came the pandemic. As it would happen, the very thing that sprouted chaos and heightened angst around the world constituted the blessing that brought stillness into my life after several years of non-stop movement. For more than two years, Chris provided sanctuary for my writing, culinary treats for my belly, and companionship my heart craved. As she, too, is a writer, we wrote in tandem, coaching one another through William Strunk and E. B. White's *Elements of Style* as we always reveled in one another's progress. Chris has been my lifeline and I will never stop finding ways to show just how much she is appreciated and loved.

As my editor, Marcia Gagliardi of Haley's Publishing was a constant teacher in the way of words and random obscure subjects. A first-time writer could not find a kinder, more encouraging ally to usher her book through to publishing. Marcia removed tarnish from sentences with the skill of an art restorer revealing the color and intent hidden beneath. I cannot understate the extent of her intelligent counsel and friendship.

Joni Praded looked at my raw and unpasteurized vignettes and remarkably took me into her fold. As my writing coach,

Joni gave me the confidence to believe in my story. She also challenged me to climb the peaks of vulnerability and view my journey through a wider set of lenses. It is through her gentle nudging that *18 Pair of Shoes* became a story of my personal journey with the walk as backdrop. She was right, of course. I appreciate her gentle persistence as I reluctantly and begrudgingly unlocked story after story of my private life.

To Katherine Burke and all the people at the Turkey Land Cove Foundation, I extend most sincere thanks. The care and attention I received while on two writing retreats offered me both physical and emotional space to dive deeply into my story while sunsets and ocean provided me much-needed spiritual grounding.

To my readers, especially the early ones, God bless you. Only a true friend could endure early writings of a novice. Cheryl Lopriore, Suzanne Ganzak Carnill, Christie Binzen, Sasha Ellsworth Dyer, Ginny Sassaman, Jack Pransky, Pamela Johnson, Cynthia Crosson, David Patrick Adams, and, of course, Chris, I lovingly note your insights and encouragement.

To Debra Ellis, copy editor, thank you for not allowing me to compromise my tone. Without your keen input, *18 Pair of Shoes* could have slowly deflated complete with flatulent sound effects. I will speculate that readers also thank you!

Carrie McDougall will never know how her frequent calls and text messages to me on the road put a bounce in my step as they countered the pull of gravity from the heart-shaped stones in my pocket.

I've enjoyed the camaraderie and regular support of a writers group. I found it invaluable to bounce ideas off one another and gain confidence to call myself a writer. A special thank you to fellow writer Amber Robidoux for her artistic skills helping to make my book photo pop with happiness.

I did not have to walk ten thousand miles to realize the tremendous importance of relationships in my life. I value my family and friends above all else and am profoundly indebted to them for supporting me throughout my life's excursions.

To Jeff Francis and Linda Wheatley, I am exceptionally grateful to you for being the mirrors that awakened me to love and adventure.

To those who have gone through the heavenly tunnel, I lovingly give thanks to my mother, Joyce, and father, Vern, and brothers-in-law Al Noyes and Richard Carroll. You left us too soon.

And, finally, to Cheryl Lopriore who has been by my side since I was five years old and never wavered in her support nor friendship, and my family Allie, Julia, Princess, Vern, Mary, Pam, and, again, Chris, I love you all to the moon and back. As Louis Armstrong noted so melodiously, "It's a wonderful world." And it's wonderful to be in it with you.

Paula plans a next day's route during the Happiness Walk.

ABOUT THE AUTHOR

Paula Francis grew up in a quintessential sixties neighborhood during the bellbottom years but, to her chagrin, not early enough to be a Woodstock hippie. With a thrifty father, a mother who struggled with depression, and a family that chased UFOs, her childhood years set the stage for spiritual seeking and pursuit of a meaningful life. Her tumultuous youth propelled her to move around the country. She eventually settled in Vermont, where she raised a family and continued a professional career in the field of developmental disabilities.

Paula always looked to improve the lot of society, and both her personal and professional lives focused on building conditions supportive of individual and community well-being. Later as executive director of a social-profit organization and then as a director within a philanthropic foundation, Paula sought to organize and lead change for improvement of service systems. With her background in addressing root causes of social conditions and results accountability, she co-founded Gross National Happiness USA in 2008.

Because of her interest in shifting the national conversation toward creating a thriving society, Paula's professional and life experiences led her to circumambulate the United States while interviewing people about what matters most in life.

Paula has three adult daughters whom she assures readers she "loves to the moon and back."

As the road continues to call to her, she has shifted to moving around the country on wheels rather than on calloused feet. Problematically, she says she remains committed to her search for the perfect doughnut.